WINS AND LOSSES

My 80 Years
On And Off
The Court

Charles Thomas Crosby

Front and back cover photos provided by Drury University Archives.

Published by Charles Thomas Crosby
Nixa, Missouri.

Printed by CreateSpace, an Amazon.com Company.

ISBN-13: 978-1537043555

Thank You

Thank you to Garl Crosby and his wife Kimie, for visiting often, for taking me out to lunch, and for helping with transportation.

Thank you to Maxine Crosby, for taking me out to lunch, and for some nice gifts.

Thank you to Judy and Richard Scheiking, for gifts at Christmas and throughout the year, and for outings for coffee and pie in the middle of the afternoon.

Thank you to Max Crosby, for so much help at so many turns in the road, including a job.

Thank you to Lloyd and Norma Crosby, for inviting me to their home so often, and for so often taking me out to lunch.

Thank you to Charley and Linda Worster, for frequent help with transportation.

Thank you to all my various employers over the years, to all my coworkers, and to my teachers and coaches.

1956 Drury Panthers

First Row: Sid Hoskins, Jim Shanahan, Charles Crosby,
                John Wolff, Phil Sandfort, Dave Shanahan.

Second Row: Coach A. L. Weiser, Larry Freund, Bob
                Kohey, Gordon Hurst, Ralph Morgan,
                Charlie Campbell, Clyde Noel.

Induction Class of 1998
Men's Basketball

Charlie Crosby
Class of 1956

Drury's first 1,000-point scorer and its first basketball player to earn NAIA All-American honors, Charlie Crosby was a member of the Drury basketball program for four years (1952-56). His 1,034 career points still ranks 30th on the Drury all-time scoring list and his single season mark of 498 points his senior campaign is 27th on the single season scoring list. The Panthers were a .500 team during his four-year career, but Charlie was far from an average player. His senior year he averaged 26.5 points per game in conference play, and was a First-Team All MCAU selection. He was nominated to join the USA Olympic All-Star team his senior year, but declined because "it would take me out of school for a couple of weeks." A native of Branson, Missouri, Charlie was a member of the Student Senate and was a "Joe College" candidate his senior year. A highly-successful high school coach in Illinois after his graduation, Charlie now resides in Forsyth, Missouri. Charlie graduated from Drury College on May 28, 1956.

From *DruryPanthers.com*

A Word From Dave Shanahan

Charlie Crosby and I met in the summer of 1941 in the small town of Branson, Missouri. That was the start of a friendship that has been ongoing for more than 75 years. Charlie was a big, strong lad and I was the skinny runt. There were a few times he had to be my protector.

As young kids we were attracted to basketball. As 7th and 8th graders, we were members of undefeated basketball teams. In our senior year in high school, our team went 35-4 and became the first team in the history of Branson High School to play in the Missouri High School State tournament. Charlie was the leading scorer.

As you will see, we did a lot together. We decided to attend Drury College in Springfield, Missouri. On a Sunday in September, we arrived on an old motor scooter. We roomed together, washed dishes together in the Commons, three meals a day, seven days a week for four years. In our sophomore year we pledged the Kappa Alpha order fraternity. We also worked together for three summers in Rochelle, Illinois, in the pea harvest.

Charlie was a hit in college and nominated for "Joe College." In our senior year we were co-captains on the basketball team. That year Charlie averaged 24.9 points per game and as a result was invited to the Olympic try-outs for the 1956 Olympic Basketball team. His number "44" was retired from Drury.

We took separate paths in 1956. Charlie took a position at Canton High School in Illinois as an assistant basketball coach, and I accepted a coaching and teaching job at Morrisville, Missouri. At Canton, Charlie was promoted to the head coaching position in his second year, where he had great success, coaching a player who would become an All-American and prolific scorer at the University of Illinois, Dave Downey.

In 1959-1960, I moved to Illinois to coach and teach. Charlie quit coaching in the 1960s and moved back to Missouri. At this point, with families and jobs, we were not as close as we had been. In the early 1980s we began to see more of one another. In 2003, Charlie was inducted in Drury's Sports Hall of Fame. In 2009, I was fortunate to enter into the same Hall. We were two "peas in a pod" most of our lives; me being the smaller pea.

We manage to visit three or four times a year. In the past three years, Charlie has written this book about his basketball career, his family, and his friends. Because of this he has become a much more confident person.

I am proud to be counted as a friend of Charlie's for more than 75 years.

Dave Shanahan

Table Of Contents

Words Of Introduction

It is not my objective to write only about myself. My name is Charles Thomas Crosby, and I am an 81-year-old man living in Southwest Missouri. I've learned that I am a descendant of Thomas Crosby, who was one of the three sons of Simon Crosby, the Immigrant. Simon Crosby immigrated to the United States in 1635, settling in Massachusetts. Thomas Crosby, my namesake, was graduated from Harvard College with a Doctor of Divinity, ranking eighth in his class of eight students. In writing about the Thomas Crosby line, we will cross over and talk or write about the other two branches when and where it is necessary or desirable. These other two branches are the Simon branch, the ancestors of Simon Percy Crosby of St. Paul, Minnesota, and the Josiah branch, which includes the ancestry of Earnest Howard Crosby, an attorney from New York. This may seem like a multitude of relatives to write about, but you must keep in mind that most Crosbys in America track back to one person, and that person is Simon Crosby, the Immigrant, of Cambridge, Massachusetts.

The main purpose of this book is to acquaint and reunite other descendants of Simon Crosby with our family here in the Midwest. The style of this book is a simple, mostly chronological retelling of a story featuring myself and my family and my friends.

Much of what I've learned of my forefathers comes from two well-known sources. One is *Two Crosby Families*, written by Simon Percy Crosby in 1912 . The other is *Simon Crosby The Emigrant: His English Ancestry And Some Of His American Descendants*, written by Eleanor Davis Crosby in 1914. I own several other books and documents related to our long history, and refer to them often for my own learning and entertainment.

Let it be known that others have attempted to write on the overall Crosby family and found it too expansive and noncorrective. I will recommend other Crosby books either about the Crosbys or written by the Crosbys. Barnes and Noble bookstores carry several of the Crosby books, as does Amazon.

From Simon Crosby up the ladder you will find three Simons and two Samuels interspersed that lead directly to Orpheus Albert Crosby, who is my great-great grandfather, then to great grandfather Cortes Fernando, then to grandfather Thomas Crosby, after whom I am named. The name Thomas dates back a ways to my primary ancestor and then on back to my English ancestry in 1440.

About 20 years ago I made up my mind that I would keep on running until I had my mental facilities cleared and cleaned up so that I could have a fair sense of reasoning. I have been running ever since I got back from Peoria, Illinois, in 1964. I started by getting a job at Mountain Grove, Missouri, as a teacher and coach. I kept myself supplied with work even during the summer months. I stayed in the Branson/Springfield area in Southwest Missouri in order to have a summer job. I even formed a circle with Kansas City and let that place be within my geographical limits of living. I knew that I had a condition called chronic fatigue and that it was going to take some time to work it out.

I should have believed more in medicine than I did. I would get medicine and take it for a short time, and if it wasn't working immediately I would discard it. Nobody told me that I would have to take medicine for several years or maybe even for the rest of my life. The biggest problem I had was talking about myself with other people. I could not talk to people or about people, nor about things, and definitely not about ideas. I just refused to talk for so long. After realizing that people have to talk about something, they really have to talk about whatever they are capable of talking about. Now, I'm learning to talk through writing.

Again, this book is not about me alone. I had several friends I will mention or talk about at one time or another. Foremost among them is Dave Shanahan, whom I have known more than 70 years. We grew up together and went off to college together, at Drury in Springfield.

It looks like I went to college three years building for the fourth, which was a good year for me. Grade-wise, I made mostly Bs, and worked at the Commons with Dave. Most of my success during that last great year was in athletics, particularly basketball. I did score as many points my senior year as I did my sophomore and junior years put together.

Dave and I did our practice teaching and drew much support from the physical education department at Central High School, in Springfield, and I thank that department for their help. They were also good about helping with athletic injuries, especially my frequent sprained ankles.

Last and not least, let me say that this book will do some paralleling with me, my siblings, my friends, and my ancestors.

My Purpose In Writing

This book has a dual purpose. One of my intentions is to help people become more acquainted with one line of the Crosby family from England through New England and now here throughout the Midwest. My other desire is to note and express appreciation for the opportunities I've had because of my association with Drury College, now Drury University. That experience played a key role in my success first as a college student, then as a basketball player, then as a coach early in my career.

My life seemed so ordinary over the years, hardly worth writing about, but my family, and my ancestry, that's a different matter. My brothers and sisters have all done well for themselves, and have over-accomplished most of their lives. They have done it all without college educations. They are all in their retirement years, or are semi-retired, and are enjoying some measure of comfort in their golden years. Many of my Crosby ancestors have achieved significance in many places and many times, and some of those individuals will be mentioned here.

For example, the Crosby family had two surgeons in the War of 1812. Eliakim Crosby, one of the two surgeons, took his shingle down and went into business. He helped build the Ohio Canal across the city of Akron, which eventually connected Akron with the mouth of Lake Erie, at Cleveland, and ended up breaking his company. He then donated his personal finances and two acres of property to support construction of the Universalist Church in Akron. The stone building featured a 100-foot tall steeple which included a three-foot gilded ball that was filled with artifacts often found in a corner stone, such as newspapers and letters and other personal mementoes. In 1851, Sojourner Truth gave her *Ain't I A Woman?* speech in that building, which was sold to a Baptist organization a few years later.

Like all of us, my story has been interrupted and interfered with several times over the decades, by injuries, a failed marriage, debilitating illnesses, professional setbacks, many of the surprises and disappointments common to us all. My injuries came many times from participation in sports and coaching. I suffered many times with sprained ankles and once with a sprained wrist, which kept me from participating in the Olympics in 1956. A pilonidal cyst the size of a lemon required an operation that kept me from entering the military. I had one serious injury in my coaching days that could have left me with a lifetime impairment. I tore my Achilles tendon, which required eight weeks in a cast and a couple of months with a cane. Before I was healed, I went prematurely into a marriage that did not work out. Before I could get to a counselor, I gave up coaching and had started and ended three full-time and three part-time jobs that did not meet our needs.

By this time, I was well fatigued, which led to a two-year separation from my wife, followed by a divorce. Some of the fatigue condition could have been a carryover from summer jobs that I worked while going to school. The jobs were in the field of agriculture, with the Del Monte and CalPac food corporations. We worked long hours, up to 14 hours a day. Luckily, there was a federal law prohibiting the corporation from working its employees more than 21 hours a day. Part of the fatigue came from my athletic participation, and especially from the tear of my Achilles tendon. However, it should be noted that during my marriage I functioned better away from home than I did at home. I ended up going to counselors, off and on, for some time. Those counselors, for the most part, were doctors of psychiatry.

I started smoking during one summer job while going to school. Working those long hours, anywhere from 12 to 15 hours per day, and sometimes longer, was exhausting. We even worked 36 hours straight on one long occasion. I did not smoke while going to school, and most of my smoking consisted of puffing more so than smoking or inhaling the cigarette. Later in life, I became dependent on smoking, but found it more exhausting than uplifting, and I had a constant sore throat. It wasn't easy to give up.

Later on, at the age of 78, I was diagnosed as having prostate cancer, which is not the worst kind of cancer, and is not necessarily life-threatening. However, it did necessitate exploratory surgery, which was followed by forty-two radiation treatments. My doctor said they got rid of the cancer, and it looks as though I got away with it for now. Unfortunately, I had a heart attack during the surgery, so I was not out of the woods yet. The medical staff was soon to find an aneurism in the aorta, which required a surgery to implant a stint.

But I'm getting ahead of myself.

Lanagan, Missouri

The Missouri town of Lanagan had lots of our relatives living there when I was young. My mother had an aunt with two sons, a sister with two sons, and a mother living there. My dad had two sisters and families with one brother plus his family. However, to make up for lost time, my dad's brother at Anderson had nine children. If you think nine is a lot of children, don't be surprised when I tell you that large families were a common occurrence in those days. Our family, my ancestors, numbered from two or three children per family all the way up to 14 children in one family.

When I was a boy, FDR was the president and a very good one, even though my dad voted Republican. My dad didn't care for the New Deal and the production lines. We had a large cabinet radio and listened to FDR and his fireside chats. I remember hearing FDR talk about the closing days of the war in Europe when the Germans were quite willing to surrender to the Allied forces, but were unwilling to surrender to the Russian army. I remember hearing about the bombing of Pearl Harbor, the declaration of war on Japan, and the dropping of the atom bomb. At last, I remember MacArthur accepting the surrender of Japan on board the USS Missouri. My dad was 39 years old, and the number of his children had disqualified him from the draft.

My dad had an eighth-grade education, and my mom finished ninth grade. This was much different from our ancestry, dating back to Simon Crosby in 1635, "the immigrant" to whom most members of the Crosby families in America can trace their roots. The Crosby line traces back to 1440, to a man named John Crosby. The ancient Crosbys were a prestigious family, dating back from my great, great grandparents, and before that, to Thomas Crosby, a Doctor of Divinity from Harvard. I should say the Crosbys are prestigious including all three branches of the family. There are several members of the family with college degrees, including me, but there are more in the other branches. However, my branch is the only branch with a completed family tree.

Being always short on education and money, there were only two books in my parents' house, a *Masonic Bible* and an old dictionary. My parents grew up at Lanagan, in McDonald County, located in the lowest southwest corner of the state. My dad was 29 years of age and my mom was 18 when they married. My dad sought work on the bridge that crossed the White River connecting Branson and Hollister. He liked doing concrete work, and would stick with it the rest of his life. He would also enter the field of remodeling, which required carpentry skills and experience. He eventually teamed up with a man named Jack Harris, who was a top-notch carpenter and farmer. My dad would later start moving whole houses after we moved to the country, just a couple of blocks outside the city limit, and one mile from downtown Branson, where I was born.

Peter And Alvenia Crosby

Floyd Peter Crosby and Alvenia Bryant were married in the late 1920s, she at the age of 18 and he at the age of 29. They were married about 60 years and owned a total of two pieces of property in that time. Our dad, who liked to be called Pete, belonged to the Masonic Lodge later in my childhood, as did two of his sons. Alvenia belonged to the Order of the Eastern Star in those later years, too. They had six of their seven children in Branson, Missouri, and raised all seven of them in Branson.

Our dad spent much of his career doing remodeling, carpentry, and concrete work, and for most of our childhoods, Mrs. Crosby, as she was known, took care of home and family. She was an excellent cook. She baked the best potato cakes, hot biscuits with gravy, and blackberries for breakfast. She could out-cook anyone when it came to vinegar pie, corn bread, ham and beans, fried potatoes, vinegar onions, and cucumbers with a pitcher of iced tea. That takes care of part of the Crosby diet. Let's not forget the fried mush and fried eggs and anything made with pork, since the Crosby family butchered pigs almost every year.

My dad frequently kept a canvas over the bed of his truck so the wind resistance would just go around anyone riding on the back of the truck.

After the Crosby children had graduated from high school, our mom started working outside the home. She worked as a cook at the hospital most of her working years, where she helped to provide for the rest of the family, as well as herself.

The Crosbys sold property to the City of Branson three different times. Once for the city water tower and West 76 Highway, then to the city for the fire station, and last to the city for a road across the Crosby property, just so they could get the fire department out west, away from the heavy traffic on West 76 Highway. Crosby Street intersects with Roark Valley Road, and is the only thing in the county today with the Crosby name on it.

The Crosbys attended the First Baptist Church in Branson the last several years of their lives. Pete and his youngest son, Garl Wayne, went fishing often in the later years of Pete's life.

There were seven children in our family, four boys and three girls, and pretty well stair-stepped. My older brother was one and a half years older than my older sister, and she was one year older than me. I was one year older than my next brother, and three years older than my next younger sister. There was more time between the last two and the rest, there being 8 to 10 to 12 years difference.

The Crosby children are, in order of birth:

Lloyd Lee Crosby, born in 1931.

Betty Jane Crosby, born in 1933.

Charles Thomas Crosby, born in 1934.

Max Crosby, born without a middle name in 1935.

Maxine Crosby, also born without a middle name in 1937.

Garl Wayne Crosby, born in 1942.

Judy Anne Crosby, born in 1945.

Floyd Peter Crosby passed away in 1990, and Alvenia Bryant Crosby died in 2008.

School Boy, 1940-1948

I remember very little before the age of six, other than a couple of incidents. My Mom baked bread. While the bread was rising one time, I got into it and ate some of the dough. I must have been around four at this time. Another thing I remember happened before I started school. We lived on a busy street heading up the hill to the grade school, and I took an egg and threw it at one of the older girls passing by after school. It must have hit her because she ran me down and swatted me three or four times. She must have been in the upper grades because she was at least twice my size. As I recall, her mother was a school teacher, Mrs. June Duvall. From then on I left her daughter alone and never again threw anything at older girls.

Around age six, we lived two blocks from the Presbyterian Church and two blocks from the women who taught the Bible school. So my mom dressed us up, my sister who was one year older than me and my brother Max, who was one year younger than me, and let us walk the two blocks to Bible class. The teacher was Mrs. Virginia Shanahan. I think I had met her son, Dave, by this time, but this was our first opportunity to spend a lot of time together. As time went on, I was in one or two more Bible classes with her and Dave, and Dave and I became friends and companions for life.

First Grade

I went to school at the Branson Elementary School. My first teacher was a fine woman named Mrs. Trout. I remember the teacher helping us to put our coats on for recess and I remember playing in the bed of sand. I can remember liking art, because I liked to draw trucks and automobiles. I remember drawing an airplane. I also liked playing basketball. I would watch the bigger boys play ball by throwing it back and forth and I would jump in between them and steal the ball.

About once or twice a month, the military would bring a convoy from Camp Chaffee in Arkansas to Fort Leonard Wood, Missouri, passing by our house, going up to the elementary school at the top of the hill. The parents along the road, which was a long hill, would gather their children in from the road and back toward the houses because the convoy was big and scary and caused a roar. That convoy must have been a few miles long. They would go by our house to the school ground to camp and to use the accommodations.

As I said, we had a large family. By first grade, I had an older brother, Lloyd, one older sister, one younger sister, and younger more sister, and one younger brother. We were pretty much a descending stair-step. There sometimes were problems with behavior around the house, and discipline, if needed, was administered at times with the hand and sometimes with a switch, usually by our mother. However, it was nothing too serious, considering all things.

Second Grade

In the second grade, I went to school one half of the year at Branson and one half of the year at Lanagan, a small community south of Anderson, Missouri. My dad was too old for the military and had too many children. He was 39 years old at this time, which was the military cut off age for drafting personnel.

Since he was too old for the military, he engaged in helping to build camps where soldiers could train. Camp Crowder was the name of the facility at Neosho, Missouri, where dad worked, only 20 miles from where we lived. This probably was the happiest few months of my younger years, as I was surrounded by relatives. I could walk no more than one block in any direction and be in view of a relative. Most of my relations on both my mom's side and my dad's side lived in this small community. There must have been close to 150 people in this entire community. If I walked south, my dad 's parents were there. If I walked east, my dad's two sisters were there. If I walked north, my great aunt was there, and just across the creek was her sister, my mom's mother, Susie Bryant. Large rocks were laid across this creek to form a pathway from one side to the other, and we crossed often.

School was more enjoyable here in Lanagan than it ever was in Branson. The WPA under Franklin Delano Roosevelt had built a school with classes through the eighth grade, and an indoor gym. This is where I learned to play and to love basketball, a sport that I would like the remainder of my life. We second graders would watch the older students during their physical education classes, and when the bell sounded, we would run out and grab a basketball and shoot it. Strangely enough, I wasn't to get out of that sneaky game without a scratch. One day, I ran out on the court and grabbed a ball. One of the eighth-grade boys knocked me down and put a knee hard on my shoulder, breaking my collar bone. This was my first athletic injury, and it pained me for several days.

I not only learned to like basketball at Lanagan. There was a family living nearby that had a beautiful daughter who I found myself stuck on. It just so happened that I had a little competition, as two or three of my cousins liked her, too. That was my first romantic injury, and it also pained me for several days.

I especially enjoyed going to school on snowy days because there was a steep hill right next to the school, and playgrounds. When it snowed, enough sleds would show up so that everyone got a ride or two down the hill at recess.

Good things don't last forever, though. They were finishing up the building program at Camp Crowder, and the Pete Crosby family moved back to Branson. We returned to the old homestead that my parents still owned.

Our dad resumed his remodeling, carpentry, and concrete work, and even took up house moving. He liked the concrete work because he learned much about concrete when he helped build the White River Bridge across Lake Taneycomo in the late 1920s. Later on, about 1948, he would build his building block factory, the first and only such plant in the county.

We lived in a valley just about three blocks from downtown Branson, and only a block or two from a couple of families that would be friends with us for the rest of my parents' lives. We visited with them frequently. The adults would play cards and the young boys would go to the attic of their house to wrestle. Their names were Ira and Julia Henderson, with their daughter, Mary Francis, who played so often with my sisters, Betty and Maxine. Mary Francis was just a few years younger than my mother, however, and she and my mother were close friends the rest of their lives.

We boys enjoyed the wrestling matches in the attic. They had a couple of mattresses on the floor up there, so we had plenty of padding and always walked away with no broken bones.

We always had plenty of popcorn and something to drink. The older people, Ira and Julia, were like mom and pop to my parents and their daughter was like a sister to my mom. The Hendersons had two sets of twins in addition to a son named Glen Glen. The daughter, Mary Francis, was a fraternal twin with one of the older boys by the name of Marvin. John and Charles Porter were the other two Henderson boys. Ray and Roy were the other two twins who were a couple years older than my older brother Lloyd. Roy and Ray were the two that we wrestled with. These years were the 1940s, during World War II. The Hendersons had two boys in the military, C. P. in Europe and Marvin in the Aleutian Islands off the coast of Alaska. When they came home on furloughs, they would dump their duffle bags downstairs in the basement, even though the bedrooms were on the first floor by the living room, with another bedroom upstairs in the attic. I can remember that cigarettes were very much in need at this time, with Camels and Lucky Strikes being the two most popular brands. C. P. was home with his duffel bag scattered all around with two or three cartons of Lucky Strikes scattered, too.

No one in our family smoked cigarettes except our dad. He also smoked a pipe and always had a can of Prince Albert on the table. Country Gentleman was the other brand of tobacco that he would alternate with Prince Albert.

As far as I know, there was very little drinking of

alcoholic beverages in our family at this particular time of my life. During the holidays, Ira Henderson would mix his Tom and Jerry cocktails and would have my parents over for a card game. My dad always enjoyed the holiday drinks, but my mom would abstain.

These years in the 1940s, I ranged from six to ten years old. I remember my dad and his carpenter friend, Jack Harris, going to Illinois to help build another military complex. I can remember him coming home when the job was completed and bringing me a baseball glove.

The Jack and Rosie Harris family was another that we used to visit regularly. These two families, counting the Hendersons, would be the two families that my family would visit with more so than any others.

Another family soon became friends. The Crosby family met the Russell family at church and we would be friends the rest of our days. These two families would let their children stay all night with the other family, which took the innermost trust. They had five stair-stepped children, too, and they had some that would match some of our family, age-wise. Plus, their socioeconomic standing and religions were similar. The Russells were the only family that had stayed all night, in reciprocity with our family. It was that way until the children were through school. Both the families treated the other children like part of their own family and vice versa.

The boys and their basketballs soon became

inseparable. The Crosby family and the Shanahan family were playing on the outdoor court up at the grade school constantly, even on Saturdays.

Right about this time, my mom was visiting with the Hendersons and had me with her for some reason. The Hendersons had an alligator box up in their yard. I was told to stay away from "Old Bill, the Alligator," but as soon as I thought it was safe, I found myself a stick and started poking the old thing. I spotted my mom coming after me with a switch, so I took off running and made it to the road, planning to run away. Mom stayed right behind me and kept yelling for me to stop running. As I neared the highway, a neighborhood boy saw me running in his direction. Being a teenager, he sized up the situation, and came out to the road and grabbed me. He held on to me, then turned me over to my mom. I don't remember whether she switched me or not, probably she did, but she seemed a little frightened, as well. As I recall, I was sometimes a little mischievous during my elementary school years, but probably no more than any of the other boys we knew.

Our dad's friend and partner, Jack Harris, was recognized as the best carpenter and the best farmer in the county. He and our dad teamed up for contracting jobs, for butchering hogs to supply meat for the year, and for the purpose of fishing. They would fish the Finley and James rivers and catch a year's supply for meal times. They would get together every week for a game of Pitch and a little popcorn. If that wasn't enough, they would come to the Crosby place for dinner, because our mom was the best cook around. Plus, she had seven children and it was a major task to get seven kids to and fro. It was usually easier for folks to come to our house.

Third Grade

I moved on from the second grade to the third grade where our teacher, Mrs. Lois Holman, taught us a lot about writing. Later in her life, she wrote a couple of good books about Kewpie dolls. As an adult, I bought my daughter a Kewpie doll at Shepherd of the Hills Farm, owned and operated at that time by Mark and Lea Trimble. Years later, I bought one of the Kewpie books and sent it to my daughter, too, with the hope that, since she had loved the doll growing up, she would appreciate the book, too.

Fourth Grade

I moved from the third grade to the fourth grade, and as I remember it, Miss Cole liked her art as well as anything. She was a calm, quiet person, and seemed to think the greater the teacher, the greater the student. We all thought she was a great teacher.

Fifth Grade

Then came fifth grade, where the students were to experience the best discipline of the day. Mrs. Bill Ellen

Hall truly was one of the best teachers of her time. She often showed the class photographs of her husband and her little boy. Her husband was in the Navy and was away at war. Mrs. Hall was strict and not one to spare the rod, not hesitating to spank pupils for even slight provocations. She would pull the pant leg against the student's leg and swat it good with a paddle, which really stung. Students liked her very much, even the ones who got spanked. She still made all us boys like her.

I was in fifth or sixth grade when my grandfather, Thomas Crosby, passed away, 11 days before Christmas, and Grandmother Crosby passed away just a few days after Christmas. I am named Charles Thomas, after my grandfather, and he was named after one of our primary ancestors called Thomas, who was named after his grandfather, Thomas Crosby, son of Simon Crosby, the Immigrant.

Sixth Grade

I moved on to the sixth grade, and we were to have one of the most popular teachers, Mrs. Mayden. Her husband was a businessman and her daughter was a cheerleader. We liked Mrs. Mayden, especially when she came out to the playground with us. As I mentioned, all the boys, including Dave Shanahan and me, liked to play basketball at recess. This was my year to move to the country, where I spent my time after school helping my dad and Jack Harris build the house we were to live in.

Most of the time I would stay on the ground level and hand up tools and materials for them to place and fasten.

At some point before opening the concrete plant, dad bought a number of pigs for fattening, which necessitated regularly picking up some garbage at a few of the businesses in town. By this time, we had moved from town to the country, where we could have a few farm animals. We had a cow for milk, plus a couple dozen chickens for eggs, and a work horse for plowing. In the end, we had 175 pigs for fattening. That's a lot of pigs.

We caught the school bus right close to the city limit sign, which read Branson, Population 1011. Branson would not start growing like it is now until the building of Table Rock Dam in the later part of the 1950s. The next boost to Taney County would come from the development of Silver Dollar City, years later.

Seventh Grade

When we moved to the farm, we lived only a mile or so from the Roark Creek. My dad would load a bunch of us into the back of his truck and go swimming. We frequently took a bar of soap with us to take a bath. Even though we had running water in our home, we still did not have an indoor bathroom. We had to heat our water with a wood cooking stove. We had to bathe in a double-sized bathing tub. I always looked forward to the sports season to begin because I was so happy to get underneath the shower at school.

We moved to this small farm where the house had
burned down, about two blocks outside the Branson city
limits. It was a house on an eight-acre plot, with a five-
acre plot just across the road that the Crosby family
would purchase a few years later. The people who
originally owned the property owned a lumber mill where
we would purchase materials for our home building. We
supplemented our materials by buying from the only
lumber yard in town, the Madry Lumber Yard. Buford
Madry was on the bank board in addition to owning the
lumber yard, and was well-liked in the community.

About this time, my older brother and I needed
transportation to get to and from our new jobs. A family
who owned a restaurant wanted two boys to work for
them. The woman knew the Crosbys were a large family,
and had approached our father about hiring us, because
he often ate his lunch there. After some disagreement
with me and my brother about the wisdom of allowing us
to go, our parents decided to let us work. We were to
work weekends only, and we would have to walk to work
if we did not have a ride. The situation dictated that we
buy bicycles, which we did. This satisfied all concerned,
especially our dad, who previously would have to leave
off work to give us rides on the days we worked. The
Western Auto store had two standard-style bikes. High-
speed bicycles had not yet come on the market. We were
just old enough and physically strong enough to handle
ourselves with the new equipment and not get ourselves
run over.

My basketball years were coming up, but not quite yet. I was playing basketball on a concrete slab that the school board had put in a couple years back. This was my seventh year of elementary education, and seventh graders could play on the eighth-grade team, assuming they were good enough. I tried out, but this wasn't to be my year. I was disappointed by having to wait.

Eighth Grade

The next year was my eighth-grade year, and I finally made it to the basketball team. This team went on to win the tournament at the end of the season, after going undefeated. My friend Dave and I were going to be fixtures on the team for three of the next four years.

Branson High, 1948-1952

The saxophone became my musical instrument
during my freshman year. By my sophomore year, I
would have to come up with $100 to keep on playing,
because my brother owned the one I had been playing. It
was time for me to find another instrument or to quit the
band, because I didn't have the money. My sister had a
discarded clarinet, but I felt that the clarinet was a female
instrument, which I didn't want to play, so I asked to be
released from band. We had the best music teacher in the
state, Tom Withers. Mr. Withers said that if I would play
the clarinet one week and give it a good try, then he
would let me go. I explained that this was a time when
sports was becoming more important to me, and Mr.
Withers was understanding. He said that I had a good
thing going with basketball. Still, I was the big loser, I
think, because his great music groups took all number
ones at state events his last year in Branson. My thanks
goes out to Mr. Withers, who built up a lot of great
traditions in Branson.

I worked at two or three other jobs during and after
my sophomore year of high school, mostly during the
summer months rather during the school year. This was

especially true during basketball season. There was no time to work after basketball practice in the evenings. I had worked at the Chapman's my freshman year, and it was difficult with everything I had going on.

During my sophomore year Lloyd was at the drugstore. I was at the Shack working with Bill Dickerson, whose dad was a sign painter. The owner of the Shack was Bob Spriggs. Bob was a personable man who had moved to Branson from Kansas. Bob also had a son named Bob, who managed the Shack. Younger Bob had a fine family with a nice wife and two lovely daughters in elementary school. Bob turned out the most unusual hamburger in town. He mixed the relish with mustard and made it into a tasty spread for the burger. He then would chop onions and spread them on the burger, which made it the best tasting burger I've ever had.

I haven't seen Billy Dickerson since then, but I understand he followed in his dad's steps by going into the sign business. I might add that Bill and I served a good root beer that customers thoroughly enjoyed. Our mugs were kept in a water cooler and were ice-cold when they were filled with root beer.

The summer of my sophomore year, I went back and worked for the Chapmans at the restaurant. This was to by my last summer there. Branson was a tourist town and tips were pretty good, so I wanted to work where I could make the most money.

I got to work at the restaurant with a person named Andy Luce, who had served in the Marine Corps. He had worked with the Chapmans before entering the military. Andy was home from the service and he really enjoyed the food business. Andy was like another big brother to me and was always a good friend. The Chapmans were good about hiring people from large families and people who really needed work. Andy had an exciting time during the summer months and had to report to the Marine Corp for his summer reserve camp. As a reserve he was obligated for several summers in a row.

Let me say a thing or two about a couple of families. The Shanahans were one of the families we were close to because we all had children about the same age. We went to church with both families. After church and after dinner, during our junior and senior years of high school, Dave and I would take John the deacon's automobile, and pick up our dates. We would go sightseeing and visit, and sometimes we would end up at one of the date's houses and visit until it was time for us to get John's car back home.

When it was time for us to visit and stay overnight, we would pick a family whose home life was more like ours. The Ernie Russell family was more like the Crosby family. Ernie even made himself available when it was time to pick a contractor to help build the Crosby house. So we used Ernie's house and two that my dad had built for an income for living.

Meanwhile, I wanted to stick with playing basketball. Unlike my seventh grade year, it differed in that we had the JOB tourney coming up at the end of the season. I would play one game at the end of the season. After having a good game, I was picked up for the junior varsity team my sophomore year. That same season I sat the bench with the varsity squad.

The JOB tourney we played at Forsyth was a basketball tournament for younger high school boys, ninth and tenth graders, and seventh and eighth graders, where I was to play two years in a row with both teams, taking me up to tenth grade.

By our junior years, it was time for me and Dave to start together on the varsity basketball team. The other starters were Bob Parnell, Perry Barnes, and Gene Austin. We had a good season with our new coach, John Chase, who was to be around for the next several sports seasons. Perry Barnes, a great basketball player who lost his life in a truck accident, never got to take advantage of the full scholarship he had accepted. Today, Willard Persinger is the only other player remaining alive from this ball team.

I was still growing. I grew from 5' 6" during my freshman year to 5' 9" during my sophomore year to 5' 11" my junior year. I was to become an outstanding basketball player my junior year. We were fortunate that we were going to have a great person as a coach, John Chase. This man was going to make quite a name for

himself. He got along well with people, belonged to a
service club, supervised a summer program , went to
summer school, and spent time with his family. He served
in the military as an officer and was also a good Christian.
He was to be my coach for the next two years. I was to
experience significant growth and development under this
man's coaching.

I would play basketball my junior year and come part
way into my being and would have to make it the rest of
the way my senior year.

My brother had left home by the end of my
sophomore year and lived in Kansas City, where he
would work for Hallmark Cards for a year before entering
the military. There he was to serve as a Navy VTD man,
next to the great Navy Seal organization.

I've talked much about my older brothers in the
family. I can't leave out my younger brother, who is just
one year younger than me. Max did not break into mine
and Lloyd's relationship all that much. It wasn't until
Lloyd graduated that Max and I built our relationship. I
kept on working my senior year, so that he and I could
keep an automobile running. Max worked for a man
named Jack at the bottling plant. Jack was good about
letting Max know when he needed him at the plant. He
used the automobile almost any time that he wanted it.
Max and I teamed up a few times after we both left high
school. We both were in Kansas City working and I had

to depend on Max for transportation to and from work several times.

Our family lived on an eight-acre strip just west of Branson, exactly one mile from downtown. Our dad had planted an orchard, and above the orchard was a big garden and a few hundred feet below or north of the orchard was a sweet potato patch.

Between the garden and the orchard there were a number of walnut trees. There were other types of trees, such as oak, elm, and persimmon. There was something unusual about these walnut trees, though. Three or four of them had wild grape vines climbing them. Even though our mom did a lot of canning from the garden and from butchering, along with some wild berries in the area, she did not care to can the wild grapes. Somebody always had to climb the trees to grab the grapes. So the wild grapes were left to the birds unless the Crosby boys got ambitious, as they often did.

Right after school was grape picking time, as long as we took a container with us and took enough grapes to the house for the rest of the family. Even though our mom liked making jelly, she didn't care for wild grape jelly, so Max and I would usually eat all the grapes before putting any in the container to take to the house.

This grape party went along fine until our dad decided to sell the walnut trees. Mr. Dewey Cole, who had moved to Branson from Anderson, where our parents were from, was a timber man who would send tree cutters in to cut the timber and then call our dad to use his wench truck to pull the timber to the flat so it could be loaded.

Most people knew Taney County was hilly country and it was a task dragging timber to a lowboy so it could be taken to a mill where it could be cut for lumber. Dewey Cole bought our walnut trees, all twenty or thirty of them. That cleared the area of the trees and ended the grape picking parties on the Crosby eight acres.

I was headed into my junior year as a starter on the high school basketball team. I was beginning to reach my stride that was to take me toward more physical and mental maturity. After having a good year in school, in and out of the classroom, I was glad to see the school year come to a close. Under our new coach, Branson probably had its first 25-win season.

Summer was here and I landed my best summer job yet. I was approached by Mac McCullan, owner of the laundry. Mac was a personable individual and was well-liked as a supervisor of people. Mac had some good people employed to help in his laundromat. I got to meet the Buckout family and Ted was one of the finest people I was to meet. My job was to deliver laundry to hotels and motels. This proved to be my most enjoyable job. I liked being outdoors driving and then spending a few minutes now and then inside. Everything went quite well even though I was to have a few frightening situations.

I had the local route that included Rockaway Beach
and Forsyth. As everyone knows, there are a lot of curvy
roads and a lot of hills in Taney County, Missouri. There
are a lot of hairpin curves between Rockaway Beach and
Forsyth. You go down a long hill and at the bottom of
the hill you run up on this sharp curve with water backing
against it. If you don't slow down to about 10 miles an
hour, you will run off the road and into the water. I
slowed my delivery truck almost down to 10, but I had to
swerve to miss a vehicle coming toward me on the wrong
side of the road. That put me on the other wrong side of
the road as I swerved and I ran off the edge of the road
and was sitting just a few feet from the water. The
bottom of my van was dragging the ground and I had two
wheels suspended in the air. I was afraid that the van
loaded with laundry was going to end up in the lake. I
went some place and called the office and talked to Mac
and described my situation. He said to go back and stay
with the van and direct traffic around it. He said he would
get a wrecker there in a few minutes. Sure enough, the
wrecker soon arrived and pulled the van to safety. There
were no highlights for this day, that's for sure, only
lowlights, unless you call watching a wrecker work a
highlight. I really didn't know whether I was still hired or
if I had been fired, but Mac was laughing when I got to
the office. He took a few minutes to help me settle down,
and things were fine.

I had another eventful day coming up not too far
away. I took a motel laundry to the right location and

somebody was waiting for me. He jumped on me, and good. He told me to look at the name on some laundry that had been delivered to him a few days earlier. He had been delivered somebody else's sheets and he could not make up the beds in his motel rooms. He insisted on checking the names on the bundles that I had for him, and also insisted that I take the packages back that belonged to someone else. He blamed me for the mistake and got a little crude with his language. Before I could get away, he was getting very personal and was blaming me for the entire incident. When I got back to the office and related the event to Mac, he got on the phone and called to offer an apology. He realized that he had jumped into a hornets nest. The only thing that could do was to listen, so we had another day with something bad happening. Who was going to predict what would happen next? After all that, I still didn't get fired. I worked up through Labor Day, then went back to high school for my senior year.

Our senior year was unforgettable, being a year unlike any of its type, a tough year of curriculum, such as physics, algebra, trigonometry, and literature. Four of the starting lettermen were back from the year before. There was a transfer student who was eligible for our sports program, George Cunningham, who enjoyed the state basketball tourney.

George was a little bigger than the rest of us who played on the team, just the right size for our center. He was here for the summer before school started and took a job working for Al's Standard service station. I would drop by and visit with him weekly and sometimes daily, to help him feel welcome in his new hometown. All of us returning lettermen were proud to have such a fine person play for our team. Besides being a good athlete, George was a personable individual who quickly made friends with the natives of the Branson area. Unfortunately, George also lost his life after graduation, and we are sorry to have lost George.

Although I was not office minded, I was elected president of the senior class, and Dr. Jim Howard was student body president. I was fortunate to be the first All-State basketball player in the history of Branson basketball. This was the first Branson team to place in the state tournament, finishing fourth after winning two games and losing two games. This was the first time John Chase went to state, but he would be the coach for three more state tournament appearances, winning two championships, one in 1955 and one in 1958.

As I said, I came from a working family, and it was expected of me that I would work. Not only me, though, because the rest of the Crosby offspring were expected to work for spending money when they became of age. I've always thought that youngsters working for spending money should be thankful for their employers.

As I indicated, my senior year was to be my best year yet. I was elected to the student council, I was playing basketball, and I was working weekends. I spent a lot of money for a high school student but I was keeping a car up and several of the high school students enjoyed it, especially after the ball games and any other times that we had group gatherings. Our basketball team went to the state playoffs for the first time in Branson's history. We ended up taking fourth place in the tournament, finishing our season with 35 wins and 4 loses.

We had chores year round, before and after school and during the summer months. While we were growing up my sister helped around the house while the boys handled the outdoor chores. Milking the cow was my brother's responsibility. Lloyd and I frequently got in on sawing logs for firewood. If anyone needed to go to town for shopping this would fall to Lloyd, who was old enough to drive. I was a freshman in high school and my brother was two and a half years older than me. Feeding the pigs would fall to any of the three of us, me, Lloyd, or our dad. When Lloyd and I went to work, that meant that dad and Max handled the chores, especially on weekends when we were needed most. Lloyd and I worked at the restaurant for the Chapmans, who had moved to Branson from Houston, Texas. Walter Chapman had worked for and retired from the railroad. With his wife, Erma, they had worked for the Harvey House restaurants for several years before they moved to Missouri. They soon opened their own restaurant in Branson. The Chapmans were true Southerners, offering Southern-fried chicken, biscuits, gravy, and hash browns.

Mr. Chapman was disabled due to a back and leg injury. He had a severe impairment that caused him to walk with a limp, with the use of a cane. Mrs. Chapman took care of the kitchen and all their employees called her Mom, and Walter was called Pop. My brother worked in the kitchen , washing dishes, and I worked in the dining room waiting on tables. After a few years Lloyd took a job working at the drug store owned by Mr. Al Alexander, his wife Helen, and their young son, Bob, who was around much of the time. Lloyd worked there for a couple of years when in high school. I worked at the restaurant through junior high and my early high school years. I was playing my brother Lloyd's saxophone and playing basketball, too. Lloyd was not athletic but he did get along with the athletes. He ran around with them on many nights after his work hours.

When I was in my teens, my dad was a great trader of different types of property. He always had an extra truck sitting around or occasionally would have an automobile that he had traded for. He would take these vehicles as a trade for jobs that he would do. He did concrete work, or would remodel houses with his friend, Jack Harris, or he would move entire buildings. He usually needed two or three trucks to move a building, along with a number of extra employees.

This variety of work helps to explain a part of his trading, except we have never figured out what he traded for the 175 pigs that he put out on our three-acre pig pen.

He planned to feed and fatten the hogs and sell them. He usually did sell the automobiles for which he had traded, but pigs? Because he needed feed for the pigs, he made a deal with the city of Branson and some restaurants to pick up their waste food. My old brother and I had ourselves a new job. Our dad usually took one of us with him to pick up the waste food, but sometimes Lloyd and I would make the rounds by ourselves.

Lloyd also got in on dad's gravel hauling operation since dad hauled his own gravel and sand out of a gravel bar out in the Kissee Mills area. Lloyd was two and a half years older than me and could handle a shovel. At least dad had a dump truck so my brother did not have to unload the gravel. Dad had a man who helped him do the shoveling after he started up his block plant. He built his own building to turn out the blocks. This worked fine until it got to be too much work, to turn out the blocks for the building industry while keeping up with the rest of his work, plus the mounting growth of chores at home. Dad decided to sell his old block machine, as manual as it was, and remodel his building for his first piece of rental property. Shortly after that he took a job with the White River Electric Company as a custodian. He decided that having a weekly income was better than being paid by the job. Our family was much happier because with the older boys were working the financial status of the family was in better shape. There was weekly money for the buying of groceries, for the children's lunches at school, and a can of Prince Albert for dad's pipe smoking. This weekly income would handle most of our necessities. The older brothers working for their spending helped the overall family needs and relationships.

By this time, Lloyd was making the saxophone sound real. I had given up the saxophone and had refused to take on the clarinet that my sister Betty had discarded. I was on my way to becoming an all-star basketball player and had little interest in musical instruments. My younger brother Max was following suit and was playing basketball and had started working at the bottling plant on Saturdays and one or two nights after school each week.

We were one of the largest families in the area, having six children with one more to come. That younger one would be a girl by the name of Judy. She became the favorite and best-liked, probably because of her being a baby. She did draw much attention from family and family friends.

I was a senior in high school when Judy was born, so I don't remember her that much in her elementary school years. I remember more in her high school years, and her participating in the band as a baton twirler. She did follow suit in the extra-curricular department. She was one of the more attractive-looking children in the Crosby family, and one of the more attractive high school girls of her day. It was a few years after Judy was married that I got reacquainted with her and her family. She is married to one of the best men that I have ever met, and she has two beautiful children, a son and daughter. She has been good about giving me gifts over the past several years. She has been a working woman over the past 40 years and recently retired from the Jack Henry company in Monett, Missouri. The Jack Henry company does software design for business offices across the country. Judy was traveling across the country helping to set up offices for software equipment.

I'm proud to say that her husband is a man of real character who just happens to be the son of a Baptist minister. Richard has been a great asset to our family and a very strong person. During the past year Richard has suffered from a back problem even after a couple of operations, including placing a stint in the spinal column. After being nearly bedfast for almost two years, Richard was up and moving around and going to church.

Drury College, 1952-1956

The first summer before going to college, I went to Kansas City to work for the Coca Cola Bottling Plant, installing vending machines. This was a very strenuous, physical job. My brothers were to go into this business later, and it was very hard work. I lived with my uncle, who worked for Coke. I saved $2 or more a week, which was just enough for school, around $50. My uncle was single and in his mid-30s or early 40s. He looked after me throughout that summer.

Being away from home, it meant finding room and board for several weeks, enough to get through the summer. Word came to us by some friends, actually my brother and a friend, LeRoy Russell, who lived there, that a certain woman at certain location would take on boarders and provide carry out lunches. This is exactly what we were looking for. The woman's name was Marge, and she was an outstanding cook, with an outstanding personality. She was our new mom away from home. We just loved her. There must have been 10 or 12 people staying at this house at 38th and Garfield, over in Kansas.

Marge did know how to be a good friend. She would pack our lunch and take messages for us during the day while we were working. My brother, who was a year younger than me, stayed at the same place and would give Jim Howard and me a ride to work while headed to his job. Jim Howard and I were the same age and were both from Branson. We rode to work with my brother until there was a shift change for my brother or for Jim and myself. When the job shift occurred, Jim and I would catch the bus just a few blocks from where we were staying for the summer. We would get a ride to and from or just take the bus as a last resort.

We didn't have much entertainment through the summer, especially since we worked the evening shift. However, since we did have one or two evenings a week off from work we could go to a movie down at one of the local theaters.

The new outdoor theater had a good show schedule for the summer. Jim and I would take in one of the more popular shows of the day. One great movie we saw was *Oklahoma*, which was the highlight of our summer entertainment.

LeRoy Russell was another good friend to the Crosby family in Kansas City during the summer, as well as a friend to family in Branson during our growing up days. This friendship between LeRoy and my brother Max was to be a lifetime friendship that would carry them into business together later on. The younger Crosbys would carry on the Crosby-Russell tradition of friendship at Branson junior high and high schools.

Our sister Maxine would meet May Jane Russell in Wichita, where they stayed in touch and visit today in their retirement years. One younger brother, Earl Wayne, would hook up with Alvie Russell and carry on with a friendship throughout their school days and throughout their work-a-day world in the Branson area after graduation from high school. Here it is 60 years later, and it is still going on with our families.

I worked through the summer and then came home to visit my family and my friend Dave Shanahan. We decided to ride to college on his scooter sometime in the next few hours. We had to take our laundry boxes with us. The rest of our baggage would have to follow us by our families. We rode until we reached a long hill, and rode up the hill to an almost standstill. I had to slide off the scooter and push it and Dave up to the top of the hill. Dave waited for me to slide back on the scooter, then he poured on the gas.

When it came time for me to choose an undergraduate school, three or four large universities offered full-ride scholarships, but people who were responsible for my mental and physical development influenced me toward Drury College in Springfield, Missouri.

Freshman Year

Before I entered Drury College in Springfield, a friend and businessman in Branson, Ben Parnell, who owned a clothing store, invited me in for a visit. He had been in the military and had spent his freshman year at Drury, and was impressed with the small school, although he finished his education at LSU. He had been discharged from the Navy as a chief petty officer. He visited with me a few minutes, then asked me to pick out a sports coat. He pulled out a pair of trousers to match the coat, then showed me a couple of ties that went well with the coat and trousers. He told me I didn't have to pay for the clothing, that it was his gift from his family to mine. I told him I was grateful.

Being an average student in high school, with a few Bs here and there, Drury decided to take me off some of these first full-ride scholarships and let me work for my keep. If I would have left engineering alone later in my college career, my transcript would have looked a little better. However, I did redeem myself some with mostly Bs at Bradley University. I even made an A in the early going.

Dave and I spent our freshman year at Drury, meeting requirements for all students. I made a C- in that first semester instead of a C+, and lost part of my scholarship. The school let me keep my work scholarship, but I had to pay for the scholarship that I lost.

Dave made better grades than me. However, he did come up short one semester in his freshman year. The required grade to keep our scholarships was a 2.6 grade point average, and we didn't quite measure up.

Both Dave and I were working in the Commons dining hall, three meals per day. We had to show up early or wait for everyone to finish before we could eat. We always had plenty to eat since the dining was family style. Our favorite meal was either Saturday or Sunday mornings, and we served ourselves. This favorite meal included large pieces of coffee cake, with spices, a large bowl of white cherries, and two sausage patties. We always got a pitcher of orange juice and a large glass of milk.

Our main job in the dining hall was to dry dishes after they came out of the washer. We had to show up three times each day, and always had to sign in and out. Everything was taken care of for school, but I still needed a little spending money. It was suggested to me that I go to a sporting goods shop at a certain location and I was to see a certain person for a job interview. I saw the right person and was hired and had plenty of spending money from then on. The sporting goods shop was called Howard & Swan. I kept my expenses fairly low, only needing a monthly haircut, along with a few other things. I was steered to what was the best barber in town and not too far from campus. A man by the name of Dusty Rhodes, a flattop specialist, would be my barber for the next four years. He was one of the most personable people I knew in my four years at Drury.

There was a funny story going around campus my freshman year. We had a blind professor at Drury who needed a seeing-eye dog or his wife to guide him to and fro. He needed a student reader to read his assignments to him. The student would write paper work on a piece of paper for him to lecture from. To his class, he would always say, "you see?" He would explain something to the class, then say "you see?" Here's the way the story goes: some boys led a dog to class, put a hat on the dog's head, then sat the dog in a seat in the back row. The blind professor would say, to what he thought was a person with a hat on, "you take that hat off." Students at Harvard would not put up with this. They would stamp their feet until the man with the hat on would leave, you see, you see.

Here I was, a freshman at Drury College, a little weak with the books and a little weak with prayer. I learned how to read better my freshman year and I liked singing the doxology in the Commons, which helped me some. Going to class is the best remedy for the average student or average reader. The second best advice is to be sure to use your dictionary.

My freshman year at Drury, we three boys from Branson would live in a large room together. Just across the hall from us were three boys from Lebanon, Dick

Duvall, Bob Colton, and a third young man whose name I've forgotten. Between the six of us, we got up to some mischief. We would use the soap cans on each other's key holes, trying to squirt soap across the room and onto the beds. We got along well with them, and would probably still be friends if we met today.

After basketball practice, I would often stay in the gym alone just to practice my shooting. I would participate at Dave's insistence in most intermural activities. Dave worked hard at getting the teams together. I liked participating in intramurals at Drury. I enjoyed fraternity participation at most events, in music, in sports, and in parades. Before participating in intramural activities, I did not care for some of the minor sports that were not varsity caliber. I learned to respect athletes in all sports, especially since I was a PE major. I did like the music contests, which our fraternity had won 14 years in a row. I would not have participated in these events had it not been for the fraternity and my friend Dave, who worked so hard at putting teams together. Dave was an inspiration to me throughout my college days.

The basketball tournament at the end of the Christmas season our freshman year was at Ottawa, Kansas. We had a good senior club and had three freshmen on the bench. The championship game against Ottawa was back and forth all the way up to the end, with just two minutes to go. At this point, Coach Weiser put me in the game. I came up with six points and two or three big rebounds. It was a matter of me being loose and the starters tightening up. We won the game by one or two points against the team that was supposed to win the whole tournament. After the game, our star guard, Bill Smith, walked into the dressing room and I overheard him say to the coach, "He is going to be a whale of a ballplayer." I overheard the remark and assumed he was referring to me.

I went to work the following weekend and asked the owner/manager if I could transfer across town. He said, "you've had a good season, so they will give you anything you want or need." That got the fire out at the time.

As the basketball season went into January, then February, we had the standings all tied up with Drury and four other schools. Believe it or not, we managed to lose the last four games of the season, ending up just one game above .500 for the season.

The summer after my freshman year at Drury, I went to Kansas City again to work, and got a job with the General Mills Feed and Flower Company. General Mills required that everyone have a union card. The work required significant physical stamina. We had to stack 25- to 100-pound sacks six or seven layers high in a tier.

Later that summer, Dave and I started working the harvest in northern Illinois for the Del Monte company, as unskilled day laborers. It was hard work and the hours were long, but we enjoyed being outside, a nice change from the class room and the gym. The sun was hot on sunny days, and if it rained we couldn't work and had to find something fun to do.

Sophomore Year

After finishing a summer of work, and after spending a week or so at home, I returned to campus.

My sophomore year was to be a little different from my freshman year, a better school year athletically and academically. My academic counselor was also my coach, A. L. Weiser, who had played basketball at Drake University, and then went to a graduate school in Ohio to become a Lutheran priest. Coach Weiser coached at Drury for 31 seasons, starting in 1927 and finishing with a 316-256 record. He was a patient man and a very good counselor, not to mention a very successful college basketball coach. As usual, he visited with me and talked my finances over with me, then helped me make out my class schedule. For the first time, my grade point average would reach respectability, a 2.6, which, again, was the minimum requirement for the scholarship.

I shared a room with a Fred Wilke, a junior college transfer, who was a good influence on me. He was a better student than I was, and he majored in math. He was a religious person, whose father was a minister. He was a big man, standing about 6' 5" and a good basketball player. He was not real quick, except when shooting his hook shot. He could flat hook it in if you hit him just right, which included timing the pass perfectly.

This was a special year for me. I was picked as a starter on the ball team seven games into the season. I had probably as good of credentials from high school athletics as anyone, but had to beat out some talented upperclassmen from the start.

During this year, I even let Patty Evertt, a very nice little gal, date me. She was pretty and smart, and, I should add, she was much more mature than me. She was cute and I liked her. We dated until the beginning of my junior year. It is still disappointing to me that she transferred out to some other school. I was the big loser in that deal. I really did care for her.

Dave also became a regular in the starting lineup in our sophomore year. Dave was not one to shoot the ball a lot, even though we would have welcomed more scoring from him. He was a good ball handler and a good team man.

It was going to be another good year. I went on to make a B+ average and keep my scholarship. The year was coming to its final quarter and it was time for track, so I went out at the invitation of the track coach, Ray Kahnel. I had never run track before, not even in high school, but I was going to run the mile. It is safe to say I never approached a 4-minute mile, and after my second season of track the next year, I gave it up.

During the summer, following the end of my sophomore season at Drury, I waited a week to 10 days and tagged up with my friends I was going back to the harvest with. One friend, by the name of Larry Gill, who got me hired by an employment office in Branson, would do the driving. We had more than 400 miles to go. We stopped in St. Louis on the way, to watch the Cardinals play a baseball game. We still had more than 200 miles to drive, and we arrived early in the morning. Where we would stay that night, we did not know. We signed up for employment and reported to a work station the next day.

We were working the harvest with Del Monte again. This time, Dave and I would be supervisors, better known as time keepers, instead of laborers or electric pitch fork people. We would go back to working those long days. The only time we could take off would be if it rained. If the supervisor was on the tractor in the field when rain started, we were to shut the equipment down and leave it in the field. We had to leave the equipment before it sank to the axle, and walk out of the field. We could walk back in when the soil was dried out and take the equipment out. Farm soil in that part of the country was rich and deep. At the end of the day, we supervisors would park our tractors and go to the farm house that was our office. That's where we did our paper work, and wrote down all the workers' times for the day. Then we collected all the paperwork to have it ready for the next day, when it would be picked up by a field supervisor.

Randy Randolph, our supervisor, was working on a graduate degree in agriculture business from Iowa State

University. We worked well together, with good equipment and with long hours. He is the one who recommended Dave and me to be time keepers or supervisors for the coming season.

Junior Year

When one harvest was out of the way, I took on another for two weeks of employment, because I wanted the extra pay. Then it was time to get home and back to school on my first free day. It was time to put my check in the bank at Branson Security and get up to Springfield for school and a little counseling from my academic advisor. I came back for my junior year of college, unaware that the experience would be filled with disaster.

This time I would ask for engineering courses, even though I knew little about it, just because I wanted to take something new. I tried engineering, but not for long. Although my counselor was convinced that I could handle the course load if I set my mind to the subject, I was tired from the long summer of work and wasn't ready to settle down and study. My roommate, Lee Henny, was a good friend who liked to play pinochle. I was ready to do anything but study, so I asked him to teach me to play. We played too much, I'm afraid.

It was time for me to pledge a fraternity, but I couldn't decide which one to join. After supper, on most days, it was time for card playing. My roommate, Lee Henry, was always ready to play, with anyone who wanted to play. It was time for me to play a bit, too, I felt, because I had been tied down all summer, working long days without much fun. However, I was elected to the student senate, where I would remain for two years. I was not political, and certainly not a politician. I was more of a peacemaker, because I tried to bring about more harmony between people and groups on campus.

As I said, this year, or this semester, was a disaster. I all but flunked out of school. For instance, I took a class in chemistry, a five-hour class, and I was skimming it. I should not have been going without researching everything, reading it all word for word. I was also working in the Commons three meals a day, playing basketball and running track.

I made enough money during the summer to carry me through most of the school year, so I was not looking for a job for spending money. I should note that my folks could not give me a penny, except they did pay for a pair of glasses one of the four years. They still had four or five children at home, and money was always tight.

My older brother, Lloyd, sent me a watch while he was in the Navy, and my younger brother, Max, working in Kansas City, sent me a few dollars from time to time during my junior and senior years.

I remember double dating with my roommate, Lee Henry, a couple of times that year. He had an automobile and we could date off campus. He was from New York but spoke more like a mid-Westerner. My sophomore roommate had a girlfriend who was from New York, also. Today, I wonder what the two of them would have thought had we known that my ancestors and relatives were from New York. I didn't know anything about my distant family at the time, though. They were all from the New England area. Ann was my friend's girlfriend, a chemistry major who always made the Dean's List. My two men friends were also regulars on the Dean's List.

I was struggling to stay in school. I had dropped engineering and was now a physical education major. I would now have to wait until the end of the year before initiation into a fraternity. Kappa Alpha Order was a fraternity with a Southern bent, flying a Confederate flag, and having Robert E. Lee as a spiritual founder. I had thought little of the Confederacy and of Lee, but I liked the men in the campus organization.

To me, liking the people in the group made the difference when choosing a fraternity. I have since realized that I don't care for Robert E. Lee as a leader, spiritual or otherwise, nor for his stand during the Civil War. He had been a good student, first in his class at West Point, and a good educator, being president of Washington and Lee College. He was a man wanting to protect his family and relatives during the Civil War. Lee said that if he had one slave, he would free him. My Republican relatives would not like him at any rate, as they did not care for him.

I assume my dad and brothers were Republicans, but I think my mom was a Democrat. When my parents moved from McDonald County to Branson, in Taney County, to work on the bridge, my mom borrowed $700 from a family of Democrats to pay for the property that they would own for the next eight or ten years. My dad and mom only had eighth-grade and ninth-grade educations, but they were never without owning their own home and property.

I didn't care for the Confederacy then, and since that time have learned to like it less. However, I still cling to my claim that it was the men of the fraternity I liked and not the Southern theme of the fraternity. I shall not forget that Fred Wilke, my good friend and roommate, thought I was losing my mind. Once more, Lee was the greater of the strategists in the war, even though Grant was the greater tactician. Lee was still up a notch or two. I personally liked Grant, because my people and ancestors were all Unionists, and that Grant represented the greater of the ideals, that the Union was more important. But, let's not fight the Civil War again at this stage in the game, even though I do like history. One of my ancestors, Josiah Crosby, gave the best account of the Civil War I have ever heard or read in his Memorial Day oration in the state of Maine. Josiah's oration can be read in full in the excellent family history, *Two Crosby Families*.

For all that I didn't like about the Confederacy and the Southern theme of the fraternity, the difference was the men who were its members. They were all men of character who came from families of character. My ancestors were from New England and had fought for the Union in the Civil War. My immediate family grew up in McDonald County in Missouri along with my grandparents. However, my great grandparents came from the East to northern Illinois, where they were married, then over to Missouri were they settled in Bates and Clay counties. My grandfather was born in Bates County and lived there for seven or eight years before moving to Cherokee County in Kansas.

Before moving from Bates County, the family had to sell their 40-acre farm, for which they had paid $1 per acre. My grandfather only lived in Kansas for a short time before his parents decided to move back to Missouri. This time they moved to McDonald County, to a small community called Coy. My great grandparents eventually died in Coy, and my grandfather then moved to another small community named Lanagan. My father was born in Coy and went to school through eighth grade at Anderson, six miles to the east down Highway 76.

Anyway, although I didn't care for the Confederacy and Southern theme of the KAs, I set that aside and enjoyed the association with the men, feeling confident that the South would not rise again. I very much enjoyed the fraternity's programs, especially the sports. We got along well together and I still think well of those men. I was fortunate because I had been an Independent on campus for two years and still made some good friends who would be supportive when I ran for office and when I played basketball.

I was shy by nature and often could not open up with people. In some cases it wasn't a matter of me not wanting to talk, but more a matter of having the right person to talk to. I seemed to fit in with my fraternity brothers. If I were to guess which political party most of them supported I would have to say Democrats, primarily, as I think would describe most of the student body. I was nonpolitical and tried to be a peacemaker in my office with the student leadership, to bring people together. I certainly was no Josiah Crosby, my ancestor from Dexter, nor an Earnest Howard Crosby from New York. Both of those men were authors and were heavily involved with the politics of their day. I have done little writing before this book, but I'm doing it now as much for therapy as anything, and certainly do not expect my words to have the impact that my more literate ancestors obtained.

During our junior year, Dave had another problem with his feet. This is the second or third time that Doctor Taylor was to help Dave with a foot problem. Dave had a foot x-ray, and was offered a special shoe which Doctor Taylor probably designed himself. The shoe had steel straps running up each side of it. This reinforcement would help hold the weight off the bone injury to the foot. This goes along with the doctor being an inventor.

These shoes supported his feet well and he was able to finish the season without further injury.

I would like to compliment Dr. Taylor at this time. He was one of a few people who entered medical school after the age of 30. He had invented a mechanical heart that was used in medical school at the University of Chicago.

Dr. Taylor also made a difference in his practice. Like most doctors, he would ask that you don't call him at night unless it is an emergency. He would go to the homes in the evenings, but only if it was an emergency. He would not charge for emergency calls, and this being the case, people would not call him unless they were very ill and had to have a doctor.

The doctor took me with him on two occasions. I was single and free to make the trips. One trip we went to St. Louis to a health conference. The meetings consisted of a group of doctors who were discussing health problems and how they could be solved.

The other trip, he wanted me to go with him to Chicago and drive his car back. He was going to pick up a Jeep that he had bought, and drive it back himself.

Senior Year

My senior year at Drury was very satisfying, especially my time with the fraternity. The KAs played a key role in my success in athletics, along with my student teacher training among the good men in the physical education department at Central High School, across the street from the Drury campus. The fraternity backed me well in my senior year. They showed up at ball games, and some would stay up at the frat house to talk about the game after we arrived home from games on the road.

I had gotten my scholarship back the first semester of my junior year, and kept it through my senior year. I felt a little flat, however, as I thought that I needed to make up a lot of the work I had not done well in previous semesters.

I broke the single game scoring record for Drury that season. Immediately after the game, one of my fraternity brothers came running out on the floor and grabbed me by the arm and said, "you have just scored 44 points, and you hold the field house record." When we went to the dressing room, the bookkeeper, the official scorer, added up the points, and he only came up with 40, so that would be the official total. The record stood until a couple of years ago, so that was sixty years or so that I was on top in that particular category.

There was another record established that year. I was on my way to score more total points than any player in the history of Drury basketball at the time, 1,034 points. My per game average my senior year was 24.9 points, which also was a record then, long before the three-point shot was introduced to the game. The total points record is not too impressive compared to modern-day players. I'm ranked in the mid-30s today, well behind Lonnie Holmes at 2,341 total points, but it is a much different sport today, not only because of the three-point line and the shot clock. We did not play as many games each season as they do today, and it is believed by many basketball people that offensive play is better today than it was in the 1950s. Single and double overtimes probably add to the higher total points today.

Even though total points and per-game averages may be higher now, it goes without saying that most things man-made have to be taken in its own day and time. There is some general thought that in the field of athletics and sports that teams are better skilled and better trained for the faster game. The philosophies of modern sports are fundamentally different to a point where teams can hold up under more competitive conditions. Scouting and recruiting strategies have gone through changes to answer the fast-paced demands placed on athletics today. Rules in most sports have changed to meet these transitions, whether it has made the games better or not. This is, of course, a matter of opinion. Either way, 24.9 points per game was a Drury record for almost 60 years.

At this point in my senior year, my grades were coming through. I was doing my practice teaching over at Central High, and I liked people such as Judd Whitlinger, Jim Ball, Ed Lechner, Jim Meintis, and Ty Thomas, the greatest group of physical education educators in this part of the country. They did help to carry me, especially since I was getting a lot of sprained ankles that year of 1956. Jim Ball grabbed me once after I had sprained my ankle, sat me down in a chair, and said, "I'll see what I can do" about my ankle. Jim seemed to know that I had sprained my ankle again, because I was limping and had just played a basketball game a few nights before. He left me sitting there, and went to the dressing room and came back with a jar of analgesic balm. He brought some padding and tape. He applied the balm to my ankle, taped it up well, with a special weave, and then he said to me, "Don't take that wrap off for two days." This meant that I would not play in that night's game in Tarkio, and Coach Weiser said we would have to wait and see about the game after that. The game that night, against Tarkio, was something special because Dave would have to play his side of the floor without me. He was not a big scorer usually, but he ended up scoring 20 points, and Drury won the game by 20 points.

I finished my senior season with a sprained ankle and a sprained wrist. I missed one game and was limited in play the next couple of games, where I was told to avoid all shooting. I had a good vertical game but no horizontal movements. I was told to stay under the basket, do some rebounding, and throw the ball out to the guards breaking for the sides of the floor. I would go into the game at the half and play the second half. I had no points for two games, which made little difference in the games, although we won by slim margins. The team played three games for the most part without their all-American, me. I did come back and scored well in the few games remaining, scoring 40 and 33 points in the last two games.

After one of my high scoring games, at Missouri Valley, a friend remarked that "Charlie plays out of his head." I did have a prolific game that night, scoring 38 points and making 18 of 21 shots, or 86 percent. It was a pretty good evening for me, and we won the game. We lost a few games my senior year by one point after me scoring high. After about 60 years, I have come across an explanation for ball players who play "out of their head." A psychology professor from Harvard said not to feel badly about people who play "out of their head," because they make such a contribution to their team. I liked learning that from that Harvard professor and book writer, because it is a reputable institution, and I had three or four ancestors who graduated from Harvard, and, of course, one was on the founding board.

Anyway, a few days later, track coach Kahnel and basketball coach Weiser decided I would have to miss both the tryouts for the upcoming Olympics in Melbourne, Australia, and the coming track season. All injuries would have to be healed before I could graduate and before they could release me. Perhaps I could have played with the likes of Bill Russell, Bob Jeangerard, and K. C. Jones, and the rest of the team that won the gold medal that Olympic year, but it was not to be. I also had to turn down an offer from the famous Phillips

Petroleum 66ers, a nationally known and respected amateur basketball team based in Bartlesville, Oklahoma. I was hurt and I was tired, and simply didn't want to play basketball anymore following my senior year.

My wrist was being medicated the last part of the season, and I don't think I was effective. I was fatigued, but no one said anything about it. The doctor, I think, should have known and done something about my relentless fatigue. My injuries did heal, eventually, but I didn't want to take any more chances with my ankles, like stepping on the edge of a step with my heal, which I've done a few times and sprained my ankle.

I wanted to break up with Patty, the girl I'd been dating for two years, but for some reason found it to be difficult. She wasn't going to think it was a good idea, so I decided to just let it be for the time, thinking I would handle it later. With the school year ending soon, I figured the time would just run out.

Coaching For Canton

As I said, my injuries healed on schedule, so it looked as though I would be released to graduate on time. A couple of my friends were good golfers, who both played on the golf team at Drury. Jim Twigger and Ron Ollis had played golf since their teens. Ron usually shot below par and had won several tournaments, and Jim was rarely more than a shot or two over par. Since they were a positive influence on me, along with Dave, who had recently taken up the game, I decided to learn to play golf, too.

When the semester finally ended, I got my clothes together and got a friend to give me a ride to Branson, where someone was waiting to let me have his automobile because he was going to buy another car, and possibly a new one. I liked the little blue sedan. It was clean as a whistle and I felt very lucky, very fortunate, to have such an acquaintance and friend as George Penn Jones. He even gave me a little time to pay for the clean little vehicle. I was planning on going back to CalPac or Del Monte, where I would pay for the Ford before leaving for Officer's Training School in Newport, Rhode Island. I had already been to Kansas City before school was out to take the examination. I passed and was very proud because several of my relatives had served in the military, and many of my friends and associates had also served. Everyone in Taney County who was a red-blooded American was supposed to serve. My high school geometry teacher, Miss Mosley, had always made the point that anyone expecting to serve their country should plan on serving in the military and gunning for officer's training.

It was about time for me to get to the golf ranch, yes, we called it the golf ranch, and get some appointments set up with the golf pro, Don Gardener. Don and his wife, Jewel, ran the pro shop and the club house. Don gave lessons and took care of the golf course. Jewel took care of the kitchen and dining area. Don also had his weekly show, a magical golf demonstration featuring unusual clubs and trick shots, for the local people and vacationers. Don had an unusual way of teaching. He could stand behind the student and have them take the club in their hands, then he would reach around them, put a back swing in and then bring the down swing in and send the ball a great distance.

Don was an Italian American who had a strong Italian accent. He had a way of making friends with people who visited, and once the friendship was made, people would travel a great distance to see him again. I met Don as an adult for the first time when I arrived to have my first lesson. I had crossed Don's path a few times as a youngster, but we didn't become friends until after I had been through college.

When I went to make my first appointment, he asked what I was doing right then. I replied that I was free for the day, so he asked if I would like my first lesson now. I already liked him and said that would be fine with me. Never having watched him give a lesson, I felt a little helpless at first, but I gained in confidence as we went along. Following that first lesson, he asked me to play the first three holes with him. After that shortened round, I made another appointment with Don. After a few more lessons, with a few more times on the greens, I would run into a person who would give me the chance of a lifetime.

This man was named Bob Welch. He was playing golf with his wife, Wivanee, and daughter, Marietta, while visiting at Branson and Rockaway Beach. Bob was a businessman who owned a supermarket and served on the school board at Canton, Illinois. After playing a couple rounds of golf, he asked me if I was interested in taking a coaching job. He had already talked to the golf pro, Don, and had gotten some of my background. I told him of my summer job not too far from his hometown, and that I would be passing through Canton within a few days. However, I told him my plan was to go into the military in the fall of the year. He wanted to know if I would stop in for an interview before making up my mind. He assured me that I would not have to take the job, even after the interview, if I still decided to enter the

military. Since he was so nice about everything, I finally
gave in and told him I would drop by for an interview
when I came through his town.

In a few days, I left for the harvest with Del Monte,
and stopped in Canton for the interview. Ben Keetsman,
the school superintendent who interviewed me, was going
to resign the following summer, but said that would not
be a problem. He offered me the job and asked me to let
them know what I had decided to do in two weeks.

I left Canton and went on to my harvesting job with
CalPack, when a few days later a man named Dick Miller
showed up from Canton. Dick was an auto dealer and
Bob Welch's son-in-law. Dick was driving a clean little car
that was a couple years old, a 1954 Plymouth, and mine
was a clean little 1951 model. Dick just happened to have
a contract from the school with him, for what was a good
starting salary, for those days. Being a good salesman,
Dick put a good pitch over on me and I signed the
contract. At the same time, he sold me that little 1954
model automobile. I finished the summer work early and
CalPac let me out of their contract so I could visit in
Canton a few days before the start of the school year.
This allowed me to meet the other coaches and school
teachers. Being there a few days early also gave me time
to find a place to live.

I was scheduled to teach four classes of junior high
geography and be assistant basketball and assistant

football coach at the high school. I struggled through my first year of teaching because I had taken no geography as a student. It was constant work for me to stay a few pages ahead of my pupils.

I was to take the sophomores in basketball, and was to lead the football team through grass drills. I had played intramural football at Drury and had some respect for the game, but we were going into high school tackle football and this was a different matter. Plus, Fulton County in Illinois was a hot-bed of high school athletics. Because I had no tackle football experience, my first few weeks were pretty much a learning situation. The fundamental drills were entirely different from eight-man flag football. It took me a few days to learn the basics of tackle football. It was difficult for me to earn much respect and show some kind of experience because I knew so little. It created a little tension with the coaching staff, even though I liked them, collectively and individually. It took a little time but I soon picked up more confidence. After football practice in the late summer and early fall, I would go inside and start my basketball practice, which I certainly looked forward to.

I was spending many of my evenings at the home of Fred Radunzel, the freshman coach and junior high shop teacher. We liked to stay up until midnight watching *The Tonight Show With Johnny Carson*. Fred had a very kind wife and the first three of what would become nine children, what would become a big family.

I was living in a two-story house with some fine farm people, the Herrings, who were parents to one of the school board members. They were also the grandparents to a junior high teacher named Ted Strode, who became my friend. Another coach, LeRoy Macklin, was also living there. The two of us had the two upstairs bedrooms, and had the run of the house, including the kitchen and the living room downstairs with a TV. I didn't like cooking, so other than the noon meal, which I ate at school, I ate most of my meals at restaurants.

My landlord had a son in the insurance business, and one working for Admiral TV manufacturing, and a daughter teaching school. They all were married and living out of town, but would come home for a visit from time to time. She was concerned about me and asked me to take a physical exam. She offered me her doctor, who lived in a nearby town. I used her doctor and he thought I was fine, except he encouraged me to get a job working outside, where I would get plenty of fresh air. Why all this? Well, this was alright. We were making progress in some direction. At least I found out that I was in need of more fresh air during my waking hours.

Canton, Illinois, was quite a distance from Branson and Springfield, 400 or so miles, so I only made the trip back home one or two times a year. I often brought Coach Macklin with me, because he was also a single man.

When it was finally time to coach basketball, Frank Whitman, the head coach and athletic director, would take the top three sophomore prospects for the varsity team. I would coach the remaining seven sophomore basketball players. We would have to use some juniors from the junior varsity to have a full practice. Eventually, I coached junior varsity along with my sophomores. This way, we could have enough players for the two teams. We did have a good year with our sophomore team, despite losing three top prospects. We went 14-4, which was our only high school team to break .500 on the season. The varsity won just six games, but they were young with three sophomores, and were very competitive. Once basketball season was over, I was left with just my junior high geography classes.

At the end of the basketball season, I went to Mr. Stark, the superintendent, to tell him I would be leaving and would like to have my resignation accepted. He wanted to know why I wanted to leave and I gave him two or three reasons, including my intent to enter military school. He said he wasn't buying my reasons for wanting to resign. He said the military can find all the people they need without me. He added that it's not all that easy to find good teachers and coaches. Why don't you do us a favor, he said, and wait until the end of the school year and then, if you want to leave, we will accept your resignation. I agreed to do as he asked.

It turned out that the varsity coach, Whitman, had all

he wanted and came to an understanding with the administration and the school board that he would not be back the following year. I waited a few days to see what the school board was going to do about hiring a head coach. They seemingly were not making a move on it. One of my coaching friends, Radunzel, made the remark to me that they must be waiting to receive my application, so I submitted my application for the head job, which I was offered and accepted.

Why he had such a high compliment for me I can only say that he had done his research. His compliment was that I would be one of the best coaches in the state in three or four years. He evidently liked the way I had handled the sophomores.

I liked where I was living but I was a little crowded. We had the TV downstairs for entertainment and for visiting. We had the kitchen with stove and refrigerator privileges. We had the upstairs with two bedrooms. Since I knew little about cooking, I ate out most of the time. The Herrings were often cheerful and greeted us frequently. Their friends the Strodes were often there during my two-year stay. Oral was on the school board and worked at the International shop. Ted came by often. Ted, myself, and a couple of other men from school went to graduate school during the summer with our carpool.

Graduate School, 1957, Western Illinois University

So it was high school out and the start of graduate school at Western Illinois after my first school year at Canton. Ted Strode was putting a carpool together with him and two other school teachers who were both science majors. He invited me to enter graduate school with them. I was to take my first two graduate courses, and I was proud when it was over because I had made two good grades.

Ted had been friendly with me throughout the school year. He had dropped by to visit with his grandparents who I was staying with several times throughout the school year. I had already planned to go to the basketball clinic at Kokomo, Indiana. I decided that I would enjoy going to graduate school even though I would be absent the first day class was to start because of the basketball clinic, which turned out to be a highlight of the year for me.

The main speaker at the clinic was a well-known coach by the name of Forddy Anderson, who had been the famous coach at Bradley and now was the famous coach at Michigan State University. He was the first coach to take two teams from different schools to the NCAA Final Four. He was an extreme fundamentalist and he demonstrated the rocker step for the coaches and was quick to use his personality wherever he could. I enjoyed the three days of the clinic and visited mainly with my coaching friends from the area around Peoria. I was looking forward to our relationships over the next few years. At the close of the clinic, Forddy Anderson addressed the coaches for his final appearance. He remarked that he hoped everyone had learned something from the sessions. He made a concluding statement that he, as the speaker, had learned a lot, that although he had recently turned 39, he was just beginning to learn. This notion of continuous learning has stayed with me to this day, as I continue to study and learn every day.

I started back to Canton but found one kindness to perform on the way home. Not far out of Kokomo, I noticed a big man who likely weighed 300 pounds with his thumb up in the air, trying to hitch a ride. I picked up the stranger who seemed to know the area and was more acquainted with the local highways than I was. I let him do the navigating because we would be riding 100 miles together. The man was on his way to Chicago. I drove a little bit out of my way but reached the point where I had to let him go. However, he was a personable individual and I enjoyed his company for the first part of my trip back to town.

I contacted Ted Strode when I arrived back in Canton and made arrangements to meet up with the college carpool the next morning. My first day in graduate school was a day to remember. It was my first day but I volunteered to answer a question for the professor. He trimmed me up good and then lectured me about democracy for the next several minutes. I was quiet for the next few class periods, and I didn't try to answer any more questions.

At the end of that first class one of my classmates approached me. He told me not to feel badly because coaches are not that professor's favorite type of students.

My next class was almost the opposite. The professor in my second class had made his assignment and I had to get it from one of my carpool friends. It turned out to be a paper in the form of a critique with a report that was to be presented on a certain date. This was fine, although I was not running on to a doctoral thesis that I could outline and make a report on. After two weeks had gone by, one of the carpool friends told me that he had a doctoral thesis that was outlined just right for a report to be made from. It had been published and was about a manmade lake in the state of Iowa.

Having grown up around Branson, I was from a lakes region so the professor was quick to approve my idea for a research project. I think he assumed that I liked the lake regions and would research a region that was nearby. By the time two weeks had passed and the professor got around to me I was pretty well prepared for what was to come. Thanks to my curiosity, I had looked up the terms that were unfamiliar to me. My paper had more to do with biology than anything else. When giving a report in graduate school, if somebody raised their hand, we had to stop talking and take the question. As you might have guessed, a biology major in the class raised her hand a few times. Fortunately, I was up on questions about terms such as thermocline and limnology, for example, and since I knew the answers so readily she left me alone for the rest of my presentation.

I remember that a part of my introductory statement included my saying that if they noticed me reading part of my report that they should not be critical. President Eisenhower recently gave his State of the Union Address and read part of his speech, too, I said. I got laughter and applause from the class from the remark, and got through the report with no other problems. Even the biology major had appeared satisfied. I got an A on my report and ended up with an A for the entire class, Elements of Research.

Canton Head Coach

My second year at Canton, I moved from the junior high to teach at the high school. I was separated from my junior high friends as a daily routine, but we got together often, including a fishing trip to Rice Lake, where we did can fishing. Who says beer cans with spouts weren't worth something? These spouts came in handy. We wrapped the staging around the spouts and hooked the hook in the cork. Rice Lake was a small reservoir at Banner, eight miles away, and was stocked well with fish. Even though it didn't have the fame of a Table Rock Lake, for example, or a Taneycomo, or a Bull Shoals, it serviced the needs of the people in the area. Fred Benson, who later became superintendent, John Ronchetto, the biology teacher, Ivan Loy, the shop teacher, Ted Strode, who became elementary principal, and I made up the fishing crew. We kept the fire going all night and ran the cans every hour or so to check for fish. As usual, we threw the small ones back and kept the larger fish. Out all night then back home the next day was our routine, and we did enjoy these short jaunts.

Also in my second year at Canton, my friend Bob Welch on the school board was planning to run for the

Illinois state senate, and Dr. Taylor was to be his campaign manager. I decided that I would get into the act. I told Bob that he should put an article in the newspaper and give a little personal history. I let him know that I wasn't much of a writer, but we would find someone to do the writing. Meanwhile, he could start thinking about what he wanted to say. He asked me if I would go and get someone to write for him. I replied that I would. Would you believe that it was an elementary school principal who had been responsible for hiring me? The school principle was most happy to see me and said he would be most happy to write the article.

So Bob had already declared his candidacy, and had put his article in the paper. The article included enough to where it could be influential, everything from his spending five years in high school up to his present and past years there at the supermarkets. Bob's son-in-law, Dick Miller, who owned the auto dealership, put a bumper sticker on my car. Later on, Dick and I drove through the main county road that carried a lot of traffic. We nailed up a lot of posters that day. We had done all we knew to do.

Now the little doctor continued his campaign with TV and radio ads. Bob won the election, beating Republican Blaine Ramsey.

My first year as head coach we should have won what we lost. I had figured out that mistakes can be made by coaches, players, or referees. When an outstanding player gets injured, it requires an unexpected rebalancing of the ball club. With a record of 17 wins and just 2 losses, one of my star players had broken a bone in his foot and needed the help of a physician. What this doctor, Dr. Bill Taylor, could come up with you wouldn't believe. The player, Dave Downey, had to sit out seven games with the injury, but we did have him back for the high school playoffs. We had to go into an overtime for having such hard luck and then a player mistake cost us an opportunity to go farther in the state playoffs, so we lost five games without our star athlete, and ended the season with 19 wins and 7 losses.

Canton is one of the great basketball towns in the state of Illinois. Our town had seen one team that took the runner-up slot in the state tournament, on an outdoor court in Kentucky back in the late 1920s. In those days, they played outside. Here it was in the late 1950s, and one of the greatest ever basketball players was to rise up, Dave Downey. He was one of the most gifted players of his time, and not just in Canton or that part of Illinois. He was to pack the Alice Ingersoll Gymnasium game after game, especially with Canton's tough school schedule. Canton probably never saw more big-name college coaches than during the Dave Downey era.

Canton had one of the best old-time gymnasiums in the area, which would seat about 3,000 people. It has been updated some but the gym is still in use today. Dave

Downey would make his mark in the old gym and would play in some memorable games. He held the school scoring record for many years. We thank Dave for his efforts, and those of his teammates, as well.

In high school, Dave averaged 21 to 24 points per game. He was an all-state player in his junior and senior years, and an all-American his final year in high school.

We had to make a road trip to East St. Louis in southern Illinois, where we split our games. I had been back from Colorado since September, and had been in basketball season since the middle of November. It was our Christmas vacation, and we were scheduled to play the biggest ball club in the state, Lincoln High School. Their center was 6' 9" and would soon join the team at Seattle University. Their forwards were 6' 4" and 6' 5" as were their guards. A tall team.

The first part of the Lincoln High game was frustrating, followed by a boring third quarter. We were about to lose our All-American, Dave Downey, to fouls toward the end of the third quarter. We were down by 20 points, so we would have to pull a surprise soon, and keep surprising them just to make a game of it. With our much smaller ball club, we came out with a full-court press and shook up the other team, right down to the last minutes of the game. We ended up losing by only four points, with our top player riding the bench the entire fourth quarter. Lincoln was the best team in the state, and good enough to beat any other team. Any time you headed south in the state of Illinois, you faced great teams.

We beat a good East St. Louis team the following night, so we saved face and got some compliments on our team from the other coaches.

We made another southern swing a few weeks later, to Paris and to Alton, where we would again split two games, winning the first night but losing the next night in Alton to the second highest rated team in the state. We lost Dave Downey again late in the game which made things difficult, not only because of his scoring ability but because of the fine defensive ability he possessed.

After visiting with several university representatives, such as Kentucky, Kansas, North Western, Memphis State, Colorado, just to name a few, Dave selected the University of Illinois, where he was to become an asset to that school on and off the court for the next four years. Dave also made quite a mark with the Fighting Illini. He set an all-time high scoring record and was an all-Big 10 player three years in a row. In 1963, he set the single-game scoring record for Illinois with 53 points against Indiana.

Graduate School, 1958, University Of Colorado

I went to summer graduate school this time at the University of Colorado. I was going to a coaching clinic and decided to take a couple more courses. There again, I made two more good grades. The clinic was comprehensive, as it covered both basketball and football. Two renowned speakers took part in the clinic. One was the former Missouri University and current Arkansas coach Frank Broils, and the other was Kansas State basketball coach Tex Winter.

I had arrived in Colorado alone, but after a short time on my first day, I was fortunate enough to meet a friend from Drury College. Burney Burton was there for his second summer. As usual, he had some fine friends that he was happy to share with me. One of those friends would be my roommate for the first term. We laughed and joked and enjoyed ourselves for the entire time. The four of us took a ride up to Pike's Peak, with the top down on the convertible. Arnie, an elementary school teacher from Texas, was the driver. My roommate, Dick, also was from Texas. We were having a good ride, enjoying the cool weather as we went up the mountain. It got so cold that we were all shivering and half way up the mountain snow started falling. That was when we decided to put the car top up. As we continued up the mountain, after another mile or so, we could look over the side of the road and down through the clouds to the long slope of the mountain. We were pleasantly surprised because none of our foursome had driven above the clouds before. When we arrived at the top of the peak, snow was falling hard. We got out of the car and soon had a snowball fight going. It only lasted a few minutes because we were so short winded. We were up at 14,000 feet and lost our breath a few times. We decided to go inside the small building for a snack and hot drink. We laughed a lot and had such a good time, more like a group of elementary school kids than graduate students.

We stayed almost an hour, then coasted back down the mountain, then back to Colorado Springs, then down the road back to Denver. We then went to Boulder, just a few miles to the north. We would have to pass up Red Rocks this trip, the big outdoor theater where we were to see *South Pacific*, one of the great outdoor plays of all time. We would pick this show up at another time. We took a different trip each week. On one trip we saw the grave of Buffalo Bill Cody plus the Coors Brewery at Golden. We drove the Trail Ridge Road, an average of 12,000 feet high with a look down to the canyon many miles away, where we spotted a train going up through the canyon valley. We saw the Royal Gorge with its deep crevices.

We saw the great Colorado River. We had a wonderful time in Colorado, not only for the fabulous scenery but also for the warm friendship between me and Burney and Arnie and Dick. Burney was a good clarinet player and fine music teacher, a real leader.

As time passed, we continued to have a good time. We went to Estes Park, where I met some friends from Canton, Illinois, and also met some new people I would hook up with later.

Soon, I headed back to Canton. It was time to get my friend, LeRoy Macklin, the football coach, and head south to Branson to visit with my parents and play a little golf on the sand greens, the golf ranch where Don and Jill still reigned high on the plateau. We were on one of the sand greens when coach Macklin suddenly dropped his club and ran off into the woods. He came back three or four minutes later with a handful of mushrooms. We took them home, where my mom prepared a helping of mushrooms just for the coach.

We stayed three days and visited with folks, including Don and Bill at the golf course, and then started the 400-mile trip back for my second year of coaching, this time as the head coach. In basketball, we lost our two good wing men to graduation the year before. We had two people coming in to replace the seniors, and I expected to have a club equal to the team the year before.

More Canton Basketball

Once back in Canton, I moved to stay with Mrs. Schnell, after staying with the Herrings the first year, who were Oral Strode's in-laws and Ted Strode's grandparents. Advantages to my living in Canton at the two different places were that I was close to downtown and actually could have walked there had I needed to. Everything went well enough and I lived at this residence for two years.

My good friend Bob Welch was following me pretty closely and sensed that I had a need to move to another location, where I could have more room and have my meals at the same time. I was enjoying staying with the elderly lady, Mrs. Schnell. Her family, most of which lived out of town, treated me like one of them, part of the family. Mrs. Schnell was a gracious person, a good cook, and she had good friends that she let me enjoy, too.

In spite of my comfortable surroundings, I was to have some miserable days. I had been to Colorado, attending basketball and football clinics, and going to summer school, as well. I had a good summer behind me and was eager to look at my basketball prospects come

September. At least I could be comfortable with my meals, and watch TV whenever I wished, and could visit with Mrs. Schnell most of the time. I was living a little farther from Fred Radunnel, the freshman coach and shop teacher. I thought highly of Fred and his wife, Ruth. I was at their house many times my first two years at Canton. I'm sure this year was a relief for Fred, Ruth, and family. We watched Johnny Carson and ate popcorn and talked very little of sports. We had a lot of laughs and many good times.

Mrs. Schnell was going to see me at my worst. After entering school for my last season as basketball coach, I was to experience a serious injury that almost incapacitated me. My famous little doctor, Dr. Taylor, put me in a cast for the next two months. I was on a cast and crutches for a while, then a cane for the next few months.

We were making progress with our basketball program, and getting ready for our first game. A school function was coming up where a little team rule breaking was involved, which caused me to have to enforce a little discipline. The result was me holding a few boys out of our first game of the season, which we ended up losing. However, losing that game because of disciplinary reasons could not have happened to a better group of boys. We did have some high-character boys on our ball club, and most of them came from families of character. Even the best of boys at a certain age will be a little mischievous sometimes, a little unruly, but, quite frankly,

I think that is good for a group of boys who want to play sports together.

We went on through the season, with several obstacles to overcome. We had already overcome some and there would be more. Somehow, the team's coach, me, broke the biggest part of his Achilles tendon, which meant a cast and a cane for several weeks. Dr. Taylor was called on once again, this time for the coach. One rule in coaching is to stay off the floor. I would say don't leave the floor, if you get on the floor to demonstrate. I did leave the floor because I was demonstrating a blocking out, jumping for the ball technique. I came down on the balls of me feet, with most of the weight on one foot, which snapped the tendon. That tendon is designed to handle 2,000 pounds of weight, so it must have had a lot of impact when I landed.

I finished out the season on a pair of crutches. When going to school to handle history class, I had to put my leg on the desk to keep circulation up in the injured leg. I wasn't working much with the books these days because I was in too much pain. I began giving a few more study periods because I couldn't even stay a few pages ahead of my students now, and I missed several days of school with the injury. The superintendent showed up at my house to ask me to try to show up for basketball practice, at least, because my assistant could not handle the basketball team alone. I let him know that I would not miss any more practices. I must have had my team spoiled. My coaching staff and I got along quite well, and my team, although a little mischievous, was the best group of boys.

My teams were reasonably good. They were rated in the top 10 at times during those two years at Canton. As head coach, this may not have been too bad. All schools were in one class, no matter their size, and we played a strong schedule. Most of the schools were larger than us, but we won many more games than we lost.

I again found myself struggling a little with my life. I would give it a bit to what would be my last year as head coach. We played the year out and I was careful not to make any major changes with the ball club. We got through the regional tournament for the second straight year. We went to play the seventh best team in the state, and we were ranked at number 14, after having been ranked number 3 at the beginning of the season. We were unlucky again, after getting off to a good first half, with a 10-point lead. We lost our lead early in the second half because our all-state player was on the bench with four fouls. He had been out of the game since two minutes before the half, after building up the big lead.

As I said before, mistakes can be made by players, coaches, and referees. Our team made two mistakes the second half and the officials made the rest of them. I had heard it said by several coaches that some officials watch the state rankings and officiate according to which team is ranked higher. Instead of saying they officiated a bad game, we would say we didn't get the breaks. We didn't get the breaks in three other games that year when playing ball clubs ranked in the top ten. Anyway, we lost the game by one point, which meant that the best team didn't win, again. This was the fourth or fifth time that happened to our ball team that season.

The team managed to make a comeback at the end of the season. We took the regional tournament for the second year in a row, and it was a dramatic finish. We had to be nice guys rather than saying that the officials lost the game for us. We said they didn't really give us a chance, didn't give us any of the breaks. To ease our pain, the opposing coach came over to say that it was a well-played game, and the best-coached game he had seen from me. He was an older man and I had a lot of respect for him.

I'm sure it was the best game he had seen from our All-American player, Dave Downey. He had just scored 33 points in less than three quarters of playing time. As I said, Dave later got his just reward with a number of offers from Division 1 schools.

We finished the season with 18 wins and 8 losses. Canton played one of the toughest schedules in all of Illinois, including several Top 10 teams that season, including facing the number one team twice.

Graduate School, 1959, Bradley University

My cast was removed several weeks later, and I finished out the school year on a cane. I had heard of a carpool planning to go to school at Bradley University in Peoria, two males and one female. One of the males was John Swearingin. The female was Judy Pschirrer, whom I would latter marry. The mother of one of my ball players related this to me, and I checked it out. After going to Colorado the previous summer, I wanted to go to a different school that was closer to my job and residence. Peoria was a little closer than the other place I had gone to school, just 30 miles away, and the three people I would ride with were all going to school during the school year. I felt like I would like to go to school with these people, so I joined their carpool and started back to graduate school once again.

Things were good for a couple of weeks, until Dr. Taylor got word of it. He called me to his office and flat out told me a thing or two. He said that I should go back to Bradley and check out of school, and to not get involved with Judy, and just go back to Springfield or

Branson and stay there for the summer. He predicted that I wouldn't be back in Canton come September, and that if I went into that marriage, I would end up going to a psychiatrist the rest of my life. Dr. Taylor was my friend, but I liked my carpool and I liked Bradley University, so I was in a real dilemma. However, I didn't say anything, and I just stayed in school.

So me and this little gal, Judy, got involved and we ended up driving her car and mine to finish up at summer school. She was having a rough time in chemistry and I was of little help, since chemistry was not one of my pets. As usual, I added two more courses of graduate school to my transcript. All of my courses were now a B, except one grade, which was an A.

I was thinking about becoming a school principal, but was a little concerned because my mind was not made up, as I didn't want to handle school discipline. I still liked coaching, and that's what I wanted to do. That was my chance of a lifetime. Unfortunately, bad news was on the way. Judy didn't like me coaching and teaching, saying that I was cut out for something else, something better, something more prestigious that paid better. She was not sure about my family, either, since she had not even met them. However, she would meet them before too much longer. I had been aligned with the Democrats and was now crossing over to the Republicans, which likely was one reason Dr. Taylor was disappointed with me. All totaled, I had worked myself into an emotional dilemma.

Marriage And Other Odd Jobs

Judy had a brother who was a bed-ridden invalid. He had been in bed since he was three years old. She had good parents, like her. Her dad, Roy, was a good worker and part-owner of the coal mine where he worked five days a week. Even though he was not supposed to use alcohol on work days, he was discreet with it. He never drank on the job, but liked a couple of beers when he got home. Personally, I thought he deserved those two beers. Her mother, Maxine, was a good woman and made sure her daughter didn't want for anything. She was also a very good cook. The family was German by nationality.

Judy was a pretty little gal and was willing to marry me, that is, if she could get me cornered, and vice versa. Even though it took a few people to get us cornered, we were going to submit.

I saw a professor friend of mine, Dr. Richard Wayland, sitting on his porch one day when I drove by. I stopped and went up to him to ask his opinion of my situation. He said that at my stage of the game, from where he stood, I was old enough to get married, and that she was a pretty little gal I was dating. Plus, you are halfway through your Master's degree, he said, so what is the worst thing that could happen if you get married and it doesn't work out? I didn't know what to say, so he said I would have to get a divorce, and that was the worst that could happen.

Now, we were going to get married and when I called home to tell my mom, she was immediately opposed. Sometime over the next few weeks, we drove to Branson and visited, and when we did, my folks kind of liked this little gal after all.

It was time for me to decide on the job at Canton regarding my coaching. I didn't feel comfortable with my teaching and had ordered a couple of volumes of history by Commager, but now worried about when was I going to read where I was comfortable enough and felt like reading. When I finished the day at school I was simply too tired and worn out and didn't want to read.

I received the volumes by Commager, but it was too late now because when I was through with a long day of teaching and coaching, I wanted to lie down for the day. I didn't feel like reading anything, much less Commager. I was the last coach to be hired, and the physical education spot was already taken. They did squeeze me out one or two classes, but they couldn't give me any more than that.

The only thing wrong with me teaching American history was that only six hours of my social studies minor was American history. The other six hours in history were

European history. I did have a free period during the school day, so it worked for me to stay a little ahead of the class. Physical education classes are always in demand and they are not always available for the head coaches. So coaches need to cooperate and carry their share of the solid core load.

If I were to teach history today, I would enjoy it much more because since going on Social Security, I've had an opportunity to do much more reading by my own choice. Over the years, as I've had time, I've read a lot history. My knowledge of my ancestry gave me some good history and genealogy. I spent time reading the history of our well-known generals when I was in Taney County. I also enjoyed *The Rise and Fall of the Third Reich*.

My family history has been quite interesting, and a little prestigious if I do say so. The known history dates back to 1635 to Simon Crosby, the immigrant, on the Crosby side of the family, and back to 1440 on my great, great grandmother's side, Joanna Shaw Crosby. Joanna was married to a Union Army officer and had 12 children. Her progeny can be traced to the Mayflower in 1620.

No less than four or five of my ancestors went to school at Harvard, and one of them was on the founding board for that great school. Another of the relatives, whose name was Thomas Crosby, was eighth in his class because there were only eight students in the class. He became a Doctor of Divinity. At some time during his ministry, he decided to sell alcohol, gun powder, and explosives to increase the offering at his church. One day he left and went to Boston on a business trip. He never returned, as far as was ever recorded.

My middle name is Thomas, as was true for many generations of my relatives, dating back to the 1900s and Sir Thomas Boor Crosby. He was a medical doctor in addition to being Lord Mayor of London.

Eventually, reluctantly, I decided to let the coaching go and take a chance on finding a job that I would like, and Judy was agreeable. I went to the superintendent and handed in my resignation. I felt good about the situation, because, considering the injury and all, I thought I had been through enough. The administrator asked me for a couple of names to consider for the job, and I had to think for a few minutes. He told me he wanted names from outside the system, because he already was aware of who was available inside the system. That made me feel good, that he would ask me for a recommendation. I saw him a few days later, and he let me know that he had followed through but that neither person I had recommended could free themselves from their current jobs.

I was taking my time. I asked for my retirement money, which would help me at that time, and I started looking for an outdoor job, where I could have more fresh air. Within days, I landed a job with a steel company where I was to work cleaning track. Right away, I liked working outside.

In hindsight, I am convinced now that I was overly fatigued at that time. We did need a little help if we were to put this marriage together. It was the month of September, and I would work here until the second semester of graduate school started at Bradley University. The work outdoors was appreciated, even though it was hand and shovel pick up work. We picked up scrap metal and threw it in a rail car so they could push it into the furnace room. It then could be thrown into a furnace, where it was melted down. It then would be poured into an ingot mold, then pushed by rail to a dock so it would be out of the way while it cooled down. It would then go into another furnace, to be heated up to a certain temperature before taking it out and through some other equipment before drawing it down, before mending it for fencing and sizing and cutting it for nails.

This was a business where 3,500 people were employed, where everyone brought their own lunch in a pail or brown paper sack. The job required real physical labor, and people had to be cautious and work with great care. The steel, when drawing down, could sometimes run out of the track and expand out of proportion. It could move up against you and leave you with severe burns. I was going to regret giving up a weekly paycheck for another type of mental activity, back in the classroom at Bradley University.

Again my wife and I would agree to resign a job as soon as it became education time at Bradley, even though it was going to take more money than we had. It was still better to go back and finish the Master's degree. We had saved enough for tuition and books. We would have to borrow money for living expenses to see us to the semester's end. We would have to borrow $1,500 to handle our simple needs.

Believe it or not, I signed up for 15 hours of graduate course work. In two or three weeks of school work, though, I realized that I was not going to keep up. I went to the department head to ask to drop some classes. He suggested that I drop two courses, and take them at another time. I was relieved, since he was the one who filled out the drop slips. I was now down to a more manageable nine hours for the semester.

I was going to have a tough time studying because we had a studio apartment, even though there was a separate kitchen. I got to read my assignments enough to pull down a few Bs, but it was always a struggle for me to finish.

About 1961, Judy turned up pregnant. We were going to have another move, and needed a place with a couple of bedrooms. We decided it was time for me to drop out of school and start working, so she was going to search the newspaper for jobs and for an apartment while I finished up the last couple weeks of the semester.

When school was out, we moved to another place, a two-bedroom house. I took a job selling heating and air conditioning equipment. They gave me a beginning draw, which was, however, a little short of our needs, but I was selling only enough to cover the draw, and would not get a bonus. Therefore, I could only stay my time out, which was one year. I knew the division manager with the Yellow Pages, Hank Meyers, who was a friend of my in-laws, and he hired me. This was a big break. It paid a few dollars more per week and I could earn some bonuses more easily with the new job. I got off to a good start, writing one of the better books in our group and one of the better books in the down-state division. We were improving our longevity job-wise. We stayed with the job for two and a quarter years, then terminated the job and started looking for a better one.

My wife was waiting for me to become a success before engaging into the marriage, so it was going to be a standoff. I had made up my mind to try one more job and if things didn't improve on the home front, I would move back to my home and call it quits with my marriage. I would have to dig myself out on my home environment. My fatigued condition was not clearing up. I hadn't been taking my medicine, and had not yet been diagnosed as a fatigued person. I would not be diagnosed for another year, but as I look back on the past happenings and events, it didn't look good.

So, I would try this next job and try to work things out

at home. In my new job, I would travel to a certain part of the state, calling on schools, selling school furniture. The company I represented would have one of the most beautiful designs and a number of educator school colors. I was privileged to work for this company, which sold some of the best, most beautiful fiberglass and plastic school furniture on the market. The material for the furniture was supplied by one of the finest companies in America. It was priced more than the average wood and steel furniture, and, unfortunately, its steel understructure, painted like bronze, was a little short on metal, often bending at the center.

On this job, I met Bob Pendergrass, who was one of the finest people I've ever worked with. He was also one of the finest salesmen I have known, and was like a brother to me.

I had not yet been diagnosed with fatigue at this time, but I could see a couple of symptoms. I would like to apologize to Bud Mackin for this. I did not make many sales that year, but I did make plenty of calls, and worked toward building up the area for the company. I worked a new territory for Bud, and his company was just barely introduced. I'm only sorry that we had to part company after twelve months. I believe that tiredness and fatigue were interchangeable. I would find out in a few weeks whether or not this was really fatigue.

One time during my married days in Peoria, I worked

a second job. My job was shoveling corn with an electric shovel at the Pabst Brewery. We would shovel corn from a box car through a perforated covering over a conveyor belt. The conveyor belt would carry the corn into the factory, where it would be processed and used to manufacture beer. The work wasn't too hard, and I was there in the cool of the evening.

I managed to work out my contract with the school equipment company. It was time to quit all this work when the marriage was needing some improvement. There was need for more intimacy in our marriage.

Sharon Collins, a friend of mine and of Judy's, who was working at Bradley University, recommended marriage counseling, and recommended a counselor duo. We immediately accepted the idea. I had gone to school at Bradley and my counselor, Dr. Perry Davis, was Freudian in thought and education. Judy, my wife, was to have an elementary educational and philosophy counselor. Well, this went on about a year, and my doctor decided that he could not help me. That's when he moved me a step or two forward, then Judy would move me three steps backwards. She did not like a Freudian doctor, even though she thought he was adequate as a psychology teacher and as a person. Unfortunately, she didn't care for him as a counselor. He said he did not believe in divorce and wouldn't recommend it because our daughter was not six years old, but only three. My daughter was only three years old. He was helping me some, but he was not helping the marriage. Her doctor was helping her but he was not helping the marriage, either. My doctor got a prescription for me, so I did have some medicine for my fatigued condition.

I did not function well in the house, but I could function quite well out of the house. We had to separate to give each other room to grow. My doctor, Dr. Davis, did admit that I was carrying some fatigue. He wanted me to take a job teaching seventh grade math. Regular teaching would stabilize me and my marriage, he said. Judy would continue going to her doctor. I taught for one year and the marriage still was not coming together, so if we were not going to make it, I was not going to stick around. I was beginning to see myself back in Springfield, Missouri. Staying in Illinois and watching the marriage continue to go down was not my cup of tea. I did love my daughter, and I loved my wife, at least part of the time. We did need togetherness where we did not have it.

We were working for some time before making a big decision like a separation, so I would have to go ahead with my teaching the seventh grade. I was enjoying my teaching from a modern math book, and I was enjoying myself.

When I was through with the school year, I was headed for a letdown. I don't know whether I had a summer job or what we had planned. I do know that we had summer pay from the school board. We had already moved to another house, one that her parents had bought as an investment. I agreed to make the move. This reverts back before the school year even started. This would be the first year after moving into the investment house, so we still were not getting along any better with each other. She did look and act more comfortable, because we were living in a house owned by her parents.

However, she called her friends almost daily. She would talk on the telephone for an hour or two at a time. My doctor called it a neurosis, that some women did this to handle an emotional build up. Whatever it was, she did call her friends or her mother every day. Her mother lived only thirty miles away, and it was like calling locally. If her mother didn't call, Judy would call someone else, maybe one of her aunts, maybe one of her friends. I had a tough time doing without my coaching at school, but I made it work with a shorter day. The doctor related to me that it was like I lost my right arm when I resigned from the coaching job, and I agreed. I'm glad the body has so much healing power, otherwise I never could have left to marry or do those other things.

Quite frankly, having our little baby girl did us both some good. With Jane Ann, we had something, someone, we both could love. It amazed me that we could come so attached, that little girl and I. I knew that leaving her would be like cutting off both arms this time. However, the arguments and constant standoffs with her mother were getting tiresome. I eventually decided we would

both be better off with me at the YMCA for a time. I was
to live there for thirty days before leaving for Springfield
or Branson, I wasn't sure which.

This little family of mine was just about my only
family. My immediate family was four hundred miles
away. I was not one to write, but would prefer to use the
telephone. Since long-distance phone calls cost money,
and I wasn't making that much money, I was limited to
how many calls I could make. I needed family help, but I
didn't have it. My brothers were in business in Kansas
City and I was getting ready to call and get some money
for the trip home.

How can you get along in a marriage if you don't give
and take? I'm just now facing this problem. The question
is, did I have the ulcer before marriage or not until after?
For sure, the migraine headaches came about after the
marriage. The doctor said I was fatigued, and he gave me
a note to give to either another doctor or a pharmacist, so
I could get some medicine.

One difference between my wife and the doctor was
that I was being pulled the opposite direction. I felt that I
was in a fish net and that I needed to leave to save my life
and to save her life, as well. I was a work-horse type of
person, and had felt that I would keep myself in work
and, given time, things would work out for the best.
Things were not working out for the better and it looked
as though I would be doing the sacrificing. We both

would have to sacrifice some, but I would be hurt over the long run, even if I did get back to my home area.

I knew I had a decent name at Drury College, even though I came from a poor social and poor financial background. At this time, I decided to get rid of my car payments so it was time to trade my station wagon in and take a used automobile from the car agency. Again, my wife rebelled, like usual. She liked new automobiles. She didn't take it so serious for long, since she had her Volkswagen. She liked new things and didn't mind charging for them, as long as she got them.

We had bought the Volkswagen after we had been married only a short time. I had married up one class, moneywise, but we, with her parents' help, were closing the gap. I wasn't planning on buying another automobile, but she was determined that we needed one. She insisted that we let her parents buy one for her. I refused, a couple of times, until she came up with the idea that we let them buy us a Volkswagen Beetle, since it would be a fuel saver. They talked with us, and in the end, I did not want to be selfish, since it was their daughter and their money. Let her have it if she insists, that was my thinking. We were going to need their help if we were going to make it together.

Judy was what they called a go-getter, and she tried to live our lives the way she did when she was still in her parents' home. She did deserve a lot, considering everything. I was going to leave because I thought it would give us both a better chance. I did not have to have the best home or the best automobile. I did not need a lot of clothes as long as I had enough. When I needed something, she would go and purchase it by charging it, that is if her parents didn't pay for it. At this stage, even though she had gone through some childhood illnesses, she was still healthier than me. She was still taking some thyroid medicine. All along the way, I was trying to protect myself and I was trying to protect her. That is what makes me say I was trying to give her a break when I left to go back to my home ground.

I also had migraine headaches and a duodenal ulcer, so I didn't see how things could be any worse.

Separation And Back To Coaching

I was staying at the YMCA, so I drove to the house and told Judy to get my papers in the office and give me my luggage. She complied and did not seem concerned. I went back to the YMCA, got packed, and left for the Ozarks. I had an automobile that was doubtful, since it was a 12-year-old oil burner with rusted out rocker panels.

It would be a few more weeks before I would go to the mental health facility, but having the teaching job would give me people to relate to. I would spend some time in my hometown, have a few more people to relate to. I also would be able to go out and maybe have a few alcoholic beverages and talk. Making small talk was one of my shortcomings. So the bar was going to serve a purpose. I was having no trouble in the classroom, and no trouble with a couple of teachers who were both single in the town where I was teaching. One was Bob White, and the other was the agriculture teacher, Phil Warren. If I could go to my hometown on weekends, I could get a couple of meals at my folks' home, and I did look forward to going out and meeting some new faces, and what better place was there than a bar.

I seemingly wasn't ready to go to church, and it would be some time before I would be ready for this, and I wasn't getting any younger. I had plenty of time to go to church, but it wasn't until later that I was to go to church and become interested in church again. It is amazing how I had gone to church most of my life, off and on, and still wasn't ready to go to church now. I actually did not have any questions on church and none of the Bible, but I would have later on. Here, as usual, I was short of knowledge and information. I was to educate myself with my reading, and my counseling would also help.

This is another reason why I decided to stick close to my hometown. Having grown up there and playing sports there, and getting my degree from a college that was well accepted, I needed to stay in society. I also knew I would have to stay out of trouble. It was a safe bet for me to go to a bar or a drinking lounge since I was not an alcoholic and I could easily find people there to relate to.

Most Freudian therapists think that emotional hurt can be reduced if it can be traced to its beginnings, so the person can experience it again and express it rather than repress it. I needed to be accepted a certain way, rejected, or justified. Freudian therapy can be good if the client is strong enough to handle it. There can be emotional problems that can be overcome without giving in to the basic course. Hypnosis can be good if the client can handle that, once he has located it. The thing that needs to be understood is that we should not go back home to our parents because they already gave the best they had to give while we were growing up. They did the best they could.

Believe it or not, I would have to go back to another counselor in Springfield after the first of the year. Here we were in September, and back in the classroom with little time assigned to me in the gym. I was to teach seventh and eighth grade math, with no physical education classes, which was my major field. The cafeteria again had good food, as most school cafeterias did in those days. I would teach to the end of the day, and coach one of my three teams after school. The other two teams I would coach in the morning, before classes started. Everyone had to be there by 6:45 and had to go through practice and be showered by 8 am. Speeding through practice and then adapting to a slowed down pace for the classroom was difficult but necessary. After school was over, I would watch football practice. When basketball started, I would go inside and tend to my business.

The superintendent of the school district, John "Tom" Staton, recommended that I throw the book away and just teach the class. After teaching a while like that, I improvised a board contest. Four or five student leaders were used. They had to choose sides according to ability to solve math problems. Four or five at a time would go to the board to work the problem. When finished, they would turn around and face the class. The teacher would declare a winner. The winning student would write a 1 in the box at the top of the board and everyone would sit down. The next group would come to the board. At this day and age, everyone should finish the problem while at the board, whether they finished first or last. We always held the contests on Friday, when students were most restless, and just waiting for school to be out. Students had stored up energy and needed to release some emotion. Walking and standing at the board and clapping for each other, even stamping their feet if their group won, would provide an outlet that allowed the necessary release of emotion in a useful way. By the end of the day they were able to leave school a little more relaxed and satisfied from the enjoyable competition. Plus, it helped their math skills, so it was a good activity.

After waiting so long, I went to the doctor after the new year, as scheduled. He gave me some little pills, which really worked. He helped me to rid myself of the ulcer. It only took a few months to heal the duodenal ulcer. Getting rid of the ulcer also got rid of my migraine headaches. I think the doctor knew that he had done me some good. As you know, an ulcer is something that doesn't heal itself. I was not one to take medicine over a period of time, preferring to just leave the pills in the medicine cabinet and forgetting about it.

I left my home in Peoria and came back to the Springfield area. Dr. Taylor, in Canton, told me not to come back to my hometown. As you know, Freudian therapists would take most things back to childhood, and claim there are only two kinds of illnesses stemming from childhood, rejection and over-protection. Either one required therapy, and they were both equally harmful. Telling people not to come back to their hometown doesn't mean there is anything wrong with hometown people.

The doctor in Peoria was not the only one to tell me to not go back to my home area, and he was saying to not go back there to teach. Believe it or not, a doctor of education at Drury College told us one day in class not to be too eager to return home to teach, since only a few would be accepted on their home ground. Dr. Clary didn't make any remarks regarding this matter.

The thing we should keep in mind is don't go back with the idea of blaming some older people for doing us wrong when they were doing the best with what they had to do with.

My life at times has been a struggle, but success is measured in different ways. Some will measure it by the amount of material goods they gather, some by the amount of spiritual health they possess, others still by the amount of mental health they enjoy. Me, I'm just happy to be alive.

I am staying in a small retirement care facility. Everyone here, with few exceptions, wants to leave. I am satisfied, at least for the time, and want to stay. I have food, shelter, medicine, and transportation. The only other thing that I have need for is books. I read a great deal. I can help my doctors and counselors to pull myself out, meaning my life, if I get the right books.

I left Peoria and got back to Springfield eight hours later. Here I was, looking for a telephone to call my family back in Peoria. When I talked to my wife, she was surprised and angry, so I told her that I was planning to stay a while and would have to get to feeling better before I would return. I said I would call her later, and we cut the call short. I got in my car and drove to Branson. I got a night's sleep and breakfast with my folks, and tagged up with a few friends. I related to my folks that I would be looking for a job, but would have to get in to Springfield and tag up at Drury to talk with my basketball coach and counselor, A. L. Weiser.

I told my coach at Drury that I had some headaches and an ulcer, and that I had picked up some medicine in Branson. I also told him that a mental health doctor would be needed, that I also intended to work and would need to find a job. He said that he had just the right doctor in mind for me.

His daughter went to a doctor who was one of the best in the business, he said, so we began making arrangements to make the appointment. I talked to the doctor the following week. He told me that he didn't have an opening at the time, but would have one after the first of the year. He said he would call me at that time.

I went back home and called my former high school superintendent, James F. Coday, to tell him that I was back in the area and looking for a job. He told me of an employment agency on the campus of a school that he attended. I went back into Springfield to Southwest Missouri State University to see one of my former coaches, Windsy Marsh. Here it was, late in August, with one week before school was to start. Coach Marsh visited with me and took me across campus to meet with another coach at the University, Jim Minitz. Coach Minitz told me where there was a junior high job in Mountain Grove, Missouri, that I probably would be interested in. I went over there immediately to interview for the job. Believe it or not, it was a job similar to the math job I had in Peoria. He told me that I would have to take all three basketball teams, the seventh, eighth, and ninth grades. He also told me that I would have one class period to coach all three teams, which meant that I had 45 minutes for the three teams.

I decided to use the old gym after school. We would have to share with the drama department because Chuck Jones, the play director, was a cooperative person and was willing to help set up a schedule for the two of us. So I would teach two of the classes in one regular class period for 45 minutes and one group after school. One team would win all our games except for one loss. The other two, who had the 45 minutes together, lost seven games each and won one game each. So you see the difference the practice time makes. Everything worked out fine for the two grades as one period first thing in the morning, looking ahead when the administration assigned the first hour each day for freshman athletics.

Bob White, the football coach, became a good friend, even though I wasn't contracted to help with football. He let me know that I could come to football practices whenever I wanted to, because after all, we did enjoy each other's company, and we did do several things together that year. He let me know that I could have the use of his refrigerator, also. I didn't offer to help with football because I wanted as short of day as possible, due to my ulcer causing me pain. However, my doctor, Dr. Clary, gave me a small pill that was to cure the ulcer, which we hoped would rid me of the migraine headaches, also. I had been nursing the ulcer with something that I had gotten from another doctor in my hometown.

Dr. Don Gann, a Doctor of Education, who did the interview, was the principal of the school in Mountain Grove. I had already been teaching in Peoria and was conditioned for a teaching job, and we would be using the same textbook. The principle offered to pay for my graduate work. He took me around and introduced me to some of the teachers and the other coaches.

A Proposal For Junior High Sports

Speaking of coaching, now is as good a place as any to mention a proposal for middle school basketball and football, based on my experience as a coach. Dimensions in sports should be resized for junior high school students. The ball could be a little smaller, one or two inches. The goal should be bigger by one or two inches, and also the goal should be lowered by one or two feet. The size of the backboard and the floor should remain the same. The three-point shooting line should be moved in to the free throw line, or 15 feet. The free throw line should be moved in by two feet, so the player will not have to throw the ball up to the basket. The three-second lane should be smaller on each side.

Who's to say these younger students can enjoy the game playing with high school rules and regulations? Winning should not be the most important thing at this age. Winning should only be important after all learning is complete, how to pass, how to shoot, how to play defense, all the skills. The second place finisher spends as much time practicing as does the winning team. Even though someone has to finish second, they need to know that, win or lose, they should play well and excel at shooting and passing and playing defense.

Junior high school football needs to be sized downward, as well, like making five yards a first down instead of ten yards, and making the ball 1.5 inches smaller in diameter.

It would be better for everyone to make the game more practical for the younger players, scale it down for them so the youngsters can enjoy the game more.

One problem with resizing the junior high facilities and changing the rules would be bigger than making alterations in a town or a county. You would have to get every state's teacher's associations committed to it, then get the National Education Association to agree to the changes. This would take some time, obviously, but it would be a worthwhile effort. The benefits to our younger players would be significant, resulting in better growth and development, and, not least, their enjoyment of the games. Anyway....

Mountain Grove, Missouri

Mountain Grove, Missouri, had a large family by the name of Douglas. There were six boys and an equal number of girls in the family. They were known as a football family in a football school in a football town.

After football came basketball, and Charley Douglas was talented enough to play any sport in the school. That may be so, but let's not get to assuming here. Charley, even with his great ability, needed special permission from the members of his family to take on a secondary sport. The Douglas family wanted the coaches to know what was not as important with them since they already had their older boys who had played collegiate football and they planned to keep that standard up. They were only willing to send their boys up after practice and before and after games.

Thanks to the Douglas family, they were a coach's dream. Any coach would consider it a privilege and a pleasure to coach for the boys in the Douglas family.

The Douglas family merely wanted the coaches to know that their sons were expected to play football and they were expected also to go to college on a football scholarship so as to pay for their education. If the coaches accepted this, the parents said, it would be alright for the sons to play lesser sports, like basketball. The coaches were not expected to bring their sons home after practices nor after games because someone from the Douglas family would always pick them up. To my knowledge, all six sons in the Douglas family went to college after high school, all on football scholarships. That family made a great contribution to college football. Both Missouri State University and Missouri University must be proud to have had the Douglas males in their football programs. Most people who know the Douglas family are proud that they obtained their educations before assuming other adult roles in society.

Now, I think the Douglas boys ought to be considered for the Missouri Sports Hall of Fame because all of them played high school and college football in the state. It only takes three brothers to qualify and they have six brothers.

While at Mountain Grove, I discovered that one of my students was hard of hearing. I used a simple test to determine how well the young man could hear by calling him by name from the front of the room. When the student failed to respond, I called the names of the four students surrounding the boy I suspected to be hard of hearing, and those four responded. Then I went to the back of the room and called the name of the person sitting farthest away from the boy. This was a simple way to determine that the boy had a problem, lacking the equipment and instruments to measure hearing ability. I was at least able to work around the problem by talking directly to him in a louder voice when the student looked right at my face. Eventually, I took the information to the principal, Tom Hicks, and we got the student to a doctor to get sized up for a hearing aid, which was better because it is uncomfortable for the rest of the class when the teacher must speak so loudly. I taught using the maxim that the quieter the teacher the quieter the students.

After teaching and coaching that first year, I got a summer job selling memberships and space for ads in a vacation guide covering the Ozarks. However, I was to work with some very good people my first year. I was putting myself in a position to work out some fatigue. I had not started working out my teaching class schedule, and would not do it until the following week. After meeting some people, I would go to look for a place to live.

I drove out of town to look at an apartment on the second floor of a farm house. I met the farmer's wife, Opal Pumpering, and, not wanting waste time, I accepted the apartment. They had one other accommodation, which they rented to another person, Phil Warren, who became my friend. The farmer, Opal's husband John, and I became good friends, too, and I got to live there for the next four years. I would also make trips back to Peoria to check on the family and would do so for several years to come. That would be part of my life that I would have to live with, along with my coaching. I would live with that anxiety for some time.

I once again would eat at the school cafeteria. I didn't have cooking facilities, but was promised the little house they were renting if it ever became available. The person renting the little house, Phil Warren, was a high school teacher who would be leaving after one year. At least, he would have cooking facilities and he did offer me the use of the refrigerator and the laundry area.

St. Agnes High, Springfield, Missouri

A new experience in education was waiting for me at St. Agnes High in Springfield, a private Catholic school, coaching freshmen and teaching PE, health, and civics. I also taught PE with the elementary classes, and helped coach the high school track team. I would take the freshmen basketball team each morning at 7. We had one hour for basketball, assuming there were no chairs out on the floor. If there were chairs on the floor, we had to take time to fold them all up and put them on the pull out storage rack.

Bill Hogue was the head basketball coach, who had two fine seasons at St. Agnes, resurrecting a lagging basketball program during his brief tenure. Bill is to be congratulated for the excellent job he did. One of Bill's greatest assets was his solid teaching of basketball fundamentals. I'm sure that the school was proud for the two years Bill served as head coach.

I coached the freshman through a good season, and took the track team, after having the cross country team in September. Word came to me that in organizing for a track team, always look first for four to six quarter milers, then you'll have all the track events covered. Then you can look for your field event people. That advice came from Speedy Collins, who coached track at Greenwood. Most people acquainted with sports around Springfield knew or had heard about Speedy Collins.

There were four highly respected priests at St. Agnes in the 1970s. Father Rynish was at Immaculate Conception Elementary School and served the system as athletic director. Father Reidy and Father Westhues were both elementary principals. Father Harry Schlitt was more or less serving an assistantship and getting ready to go to San Francisco to develop a radio and television ministry. These men were outstanding individuals and you had to wonder how Catholic High School would ever survive without them.

Mine was an experimental year at St. Agnes, and my contract terminated. So, I closed my books and headed back to Branson for the summer. I spent the summer working in the land business, selling property lots in development.

Kansas City And Back

Then I would head to Kansas City, where I would work for R. L. Polk & Company, selling city directories. I worked at this for a few weeks, then went back to Branson and worked selling property at a couple of land developments.

After the fall of the year rolled around, I headed back to Kansas City, where I would work for the next several years. I started with Yellow Freight Trucking as a dock supervisor, a job that lasted eight months. When the time for cuts came, the last person hired would be the first to go, so I went and spent the next few months substituting for teachers in the Kansas City area. I did this for one term, then insisted on staying with some work where I could have plenty of outdoor time, because that was better for my health.

My next job would be for my brother in the vending business. I would make special deliveries, go after needed supplies and beverages, and be their errand boy. This was the best-paying job that I was to have yet, grossing me $10,000 for the year.

At the end of the year, I was looking for another job. I hired on with Foremost Dairy, filling vending machines with ice cream bars and boxed pints of ice cream. I spent one week in training, then started on the job that no one else wanted. I enjoyed the job because I got to work outside, even though I did more than was expected and worked 20 hours straight on some days. I delivered more ice cream than had ever been delivered in the winter months. I made more money than had ever been made by a winter delivery man, the most in the history of the Foremost company. This job lasted six months through the winter, until I had to give way to a union employee who would take the job through the summer. That job would take someone in good health who could fill a certain number of machines whether they were half full or fully loaded.

Since I was out of work once again, and because I was tired of the city, I headed back to the Ozarks to work in the land and vacationing industry. I worked at Shepherd of the Hills Theater at night two summers in a row, and took unemployment twice in a two-year span. That old fatigue was still with me, so I needed to stay outside. I then worked for Silver Dollar City for two summer seasons in a row, and took unemployment twice more.

The next go round, I worked for Wilco Enterprises, selling land. I was having quite a hard time, going around with a bad case of fatigue. Believe it or not, I wasn't taking any medicine all this time. I should have been taking it for all those years, but for the most part, I would not take any medicine very long at a time. If I had a bottle of pills, I usually took a few and then I would set it in the back of the cabinet and forget it. For the past 15 years, though, I have taken my medicine regularly, and it evidently has done me some good.

I was fortunate to have had understanding employers, Pete and Jack Herschend for my part-time job at Silver Dollar City, the Trimble family at Shepherd of the Hills, and Harold Epps at Wilco Enterprises.

I went to Unity Church in the 1970s and lived with a doctor friend, Dr. Joe Price, and his wife, Marge. I have recently read a number of small books on Christianity, Protestantism, and Evangelism, including the pamphlet *Our Daily Bread* from RBC Ministries in Grand Rapids. I got some good information on Fanny Crosby from RBC Ministries. I also have a DVD recording of ten Fanny Crosby hymns.

A doctor friend of mine told me that Unity was regarded by some as a cult. It was for that reason, plus the fact that they believe everything was spirit, that caused me to return to my previous Protestant group. Unity follows some of the teachings of the Fillmore family. As I understand it, the Fillmores were primarily a prayer group for meditation, but they declared themselves a church primarily for tax purposes.

The Unitarians are a denomination that moved from

England to New England years ago. The Unitarians believe in the Trinity as a whole, but not as separate identities. Several members of the Simon Crosby branch of the family believed in Unitarianism. The Pete Crosby family, my family, came from the Thomas Crosby branch which was primarily a group of Protestants.

I have spent some time with Unity in Lee's Summit, Missouri, and don't know that I would call them a cult. Unity's teaching are metaphysical and very interesting. They accept many metaphysical authors and carry their books in the Unity bookstores. I have read a number of these books, and some have been on the best-seller lists. Unity authors have turned out several good books, many of which are based on the teachings of the Fillmores, or on the lives of the Fillmores. Some of the Crosbys from New England belonged to Unity and called themselves Unitarians. The name Unitarian came to this country from England. Unitarians do not separate the Godhead. However, to my knowledge, the Unitarians believe in the Father, the Son, and the Holy Ghost or Spirit, which to me means that Unitarians should be regarded as Christians.

Unity in Lee's Summit believes in a Christ within but do not say whether or not they are Christians. Unity does not belong to the Ecumenical Council. To my knowledge, you have to believe in the Father, the Son, and the Holy Ghost as separate entities before being accepted into the Ecumenical Council. In the last analysis, I would say that

Unity and Unitarians are not one and the same.

The Mormons at Salt Lake City, the followers of Joseph Smith, are considered by some to be a cult. If you were to go by the strictness of the term and say a Christian belief is one by which their church is a Christ-centered church, which is saying a non-Christian church must be a cult. Since the full name of the Mormon church is the Church of Jesus Christ of Latter-Day Saints and their scriptures are filled with stories of Christ and his life, I would consider them to be a Christian organization, too.

In my past, some of my relatives belonged to the Latter-Day Saints. As a matter of fact, three first cousins and two second cousins belong to the LDS church out West. Most of my ancestry were Protestants. The Crosbys in this country can all be traced back to Simon Crosby, the Immigrant.

The Thomas Crosby branch of the family is my line. Thomas was one of the three sons of Simon Crosby, and was probably a Protestant, as was his father, who was looking for religious freedom in this country. Thomas earned a Doctor of Divinity from Harvard and carried on with an unusual ministry.

Many Crosby families in America can trace back to Simon Crosby, but not all. Bing Crosby's family, for example, came from Ireland to Canada, then to the state of Washington.

I had a grandfather Crosby who was a Methodist living in Lanagan, Missouri. My parents, Pete and Alvenia, were members of the Assemblies of God church in my childhood and adolescence living in Branson. They became Baptists in their later years, along with my younger sister Judy and her husband, Richard Schiehinge. Richard's father was a Baptist minister.

Judy, our youngest sister, was probably the best Christian in our family, other than our mother, and has been well-respected as a member of our family. Her husband Richard is of equal status, an outstanding example of Christianity.

Personally, I claim to be a Christian of the nondenominational type, what some call an Independent Protestant. I like meditation and spiritual music. I like the Lord's prayer and Psalm 23. I also like a few other pieces of instrumental verses. I would not like a lot of sacraments because it would be too binding a system and too restrictive of my life. I like life to be a little less structured, even though I do like my days to be orderly. I do not like being in a straightjacket.

I sometimes revert to the doxology when time is short, or the Lord's prayer, or Psalms 23. I like keeping a hymn book close by so I can read or sing a song, or a hymn book when I need to take on something spiritual. I like Fanny Crosby's *Ten Hymns*, published by RBC Ministries, in Grand Rapids, Michigan, and it only takes a few minutes to play on a DVD. Her *Redeemed* is one of my favorites.

Here is a short prayer used when you are tired or short of time, or when someone is in the hospital:

Now I lay me down to sleep,
I pray the Lord my soul to keep.
If I should die before I wake,
I pray the Lord my soul to take.

If you are a babe in Christ, or are a little immature as a Christian, take a look at this for God's guide, in this order: the word, the Holy Bible; the spirit, the Holy Ghost; the people, God's people; conscience, the subjective or inner self.

If you need a formula for prayer, you may benefit from ACTS:

A = adore
C = confess
T = thanksgiving
S = supplication

This is an institutional prayer used by a religious organization. If you wish, you may add a P to the beginning, for praise, and it becomes PACTS. You can change the A to ask, and you have a different prayer.

Consider these four levels of consciousness:

Beta   =   awareness
Alpha   =   semi-drowsy awareness
Theta   =   deep, drowsy awareness
Delta   =   deep sleep

Theta is a level of consciousness where we meet God or the meditative level. Man introduces himself through scripture where God does the talking. In prayer, man does the talking.

Passionate love is an experience invoking feelings of euphoria, intimacy, and intense sexual attraction.

Compassionate love is an experience invoking affection, trust, and concern for a partner's well-being.

Agape love is God's love, or true charity. The difference between Christianity and other religions is the separation of religion and government.

If I had to live in Taney County, Missouri, I would probably live as a Protestant and probably as an independent. This being a truth about my overall philosophy, I still like some Democrats, and I do admire some Catholics, which I have for the past several years.

I have liked the Catholic priests as well as the Episcopalian priests and members of the Episcopal Church. I happen to like so many people in my home county that I frequently cross lines: religious lines, political lines, economic lines, educational lines. I cross political lines because I like Democrats in local government, meaning city offices, school boards, and in business. I like Republicans in county offices, but with prosecuting attorney going to the Democrats and a fair share of the business going to Republicans.

I was reared in a split political family, with my dad voting Republican and my mom going for the Democrats. I worked for Democratic employers much of the time when growing up in Branson. I'm sure that I have let national trends in high offices influence me down through the years. I'm glad I never ran for public office because I needed to be where I could enjoy people. I liked people regardless of their religious, political, or economic philosophies. I participated in sports growing up, and played on teams in Branson that had more parents who were Democrats than Republicans. However, my last two years in high school, the coach was a Republican and a man of large stature. He was well-liked and could have run for office on any level and have won.

Should it be that I not go back to my hometown because I like too many people in too many walks of life? I like people who were poor people back when I was growing up. My parents were poor people and they believed in hard work and producing as much food as possible by having a cow for milk, cheese, and butter, a few chickens for eggs, and a horse for plowing. They always wanted their garden to have a specialty crop, such as sweet potatoes, in the bottom field and a few hogs for butchering. We had plenty of pork but had to buy our beef.

Even though it was in a different part of the country in a different state, I got to help pay my Democratic employers back. I got to help get a Democrat elected in Canton, Illinois, and he was able to get some legislation passed that provided housing for the elderly, among other things.

I do have some big questions. What would I be good at? What kind of work would I like to be doing? Am I a person with compassion? Would I like bugging out altogether? I would like bugging out altogether unless there is something I would like doing.

I have picked up a new interest. I like writing. I have to wonder how long it will last, but I hope I continue to write as I find it has a therapeutic effect on me. I'm happy for one teacher in the Simon Crosby branch, a woman named May Crosby. She got her degree and taught school for eight years. She then worked for the government for eight years. She wanted to work to satisfy her humanitarian need. She felt that she was a humanitarian and wanted to work with children. She applied for a job teaching school on the Dawes Reservation in the Little Big Horn area in Montana. She satisfied her need to be of service for three years. She returned to her hometown of Dexter, Maine, where she taught and retired. A few years later, in 1901, she was married to Alphens B. Stickney of St. Paul, Minnesota, president of the Chicago Great Western Railroad. They resided in their palatial Summit Avenue home in St. Paul. Mr. Stickney was born in Maine and spent his early boyhood days there. He was a law student in Josiah Crosby's office. He was the son of Daniel Stickney, a well-known newspaper editor in Aroostook County.

At this point, I would like to say that I have had a lot of time to read since being on Supplementary Security Income and then on Social Security. When in Branson, I was too far from the library, and later, after my burn out from fatigue, I was moved to Forsyth and placed under a guardianship. There was a library just a few blocks away so I got to read some books. I primarily read books about famous generals, such as Grant, Patton, Napoleon, MacArthur, Alexander, the Great. I read a few other books, such as *The Rise and Fall of the Third Reich*, and *Sports in America*. I also read books on the Russo-Japanese War, submarines in the Pacific, and the Civil War. All that reading was the beginning of my personal research into my history, which led to my study of religion, which turned into my study of psychology.

I am presently reading, for the second time, *Reading For Thinking* by Laraine Flemming, after rereading most of the articles two or three times. I am reading a good psychology book by three Harvard professors, Schacter, Gilbert, and Wegner. I have read several books on metaphysics while visiting Unity School of Christianity. I've read no less than a dozen authors on metaphysics.

As I sit here writing this book, I have to think of how fortunate I am. I enjoy reading much more in my old age than I did in my younger years. I was more of an audio learner than I was a visual learner and I didn't care that much for kinesthetic learning, especially putting puzzles together. However, I did the listening in a classroom setting.

These Days, 2016

I don't mind admitting that I like having a guardian, and I plan on keeping one for some time to come. As it was when I was a young man, I don't care to cook my own meals. I've never liked to keep a doctor to prescribe medicine, and I rarely take my medicine after two or three weeks. I do like paying my bills, though. As long as I have shelter and food, as long as I have medicine, as long as I have transportation for shopping, as long as I have my books, I am satisfied. As long as I have a guardian, someone who cares about me, someone who will take care of my personal needs, someone who will take care of things like insurance, I am content. I don't mind not having an automobile as long as I can arrange a ride for a little shopping or an occasional outing.

I am writing a book and I am using a few books of my own, plus a few from the library. I am satisfied with my writing, and I am told that it is good. I feel it is good enough and it pleases me.

There are some advantages to being in a care facility. You can get help paying for psychiatric care. It is easier to take medicine daily because they don't let you forget it. Our facility has its own doctor, so the doctor comes to me.

I don't like admitting that I have an unsound mind, but I do like having a guardian. I don't like cooking, so I get my meals provided, plus a few snacks, if I have a sealed container. They provide transportation as long as you are going to get medical attention. Thanks to my family, mostly my brother Floyd, I get regular rides for shopping and for pleasure, plus he often takes me out for a meal. My friends Dave and Phil Shanahan also take me out for dinner whenever they are in town.

Other small advantages of institutional care are that you get your laundry done and you get your room cleaned daily. They do believe in cleaning. They require you to take a shower every day or two. These things seem small for people who have their freedom and have their own homes, but they are big things for people who are ill and need more help.

Medicare and Medicaid are two large items and something that the entire country should be proud of. We have LBJ to thank for these two methods of insurance. I have to wonder how much crime has been reduced by these two social services. I am only sorry that dental service had to be dropped, but it is understandable that the costs run higher than federal or state budgets will allow. The only option was to drop it.

Why do I say that I may keep a guardian for some time to come? Some people in the healthcare service will tell you it's like a jungle out there. We must admit that if some people are on the street, without food or shelter, then it could very well seem like a jungle out there. Then it's time to look for a Victory Mission or a Salvation Army, or find a church or other charity organization that contributes to the welfare of others.

At this point, I think it is proper to mention one of the greatest mission workers of all time, Fanny Crosby, who was known as the Queen of the Gospel Song Writers. My family claims relation to her, even though the relationship is distant. We are proud of her. Francis Jane Crosby was born March 24, 1820, in Brewster, New York. She wrote more than 9,000 hymns, some of which are among the most popular faiths. She believed that her hymns would bring people to Christ. She was committed to rescue missions and was known for her public speaking abilities. The most remarkable thing about her is that she accomplished so much despite being blind. Fanny Crosby has generally been represented by the largest number of hymns of all the twentieth century hymnals. Some of her best-known songs include *Blessed Assurance, Pass Me Not, Gentle Savior, Jesus Is Tenderly Calling You Home, Praise Him Praise Him*, and *Rescue The Perishing*. Fanny Crosby also wrote more than 1,000 poems, many of which were published in her four books, which can be found in libraries and bookstores across the country and online. Fanny died February 13, 1915, at age 95.

I have enjoyed introducing and mentioning my ancestors in this book. They are a prestigious family and I think readers will enjoy learning about them, and perhaps develop a desire to learn more about them from other books.

As a young man, my family history could have been an inspiration to me, but I did not have the information, the genealogy or history of my family. Today, I know about my family tree and have some books about some of the branches.

Oliver Crosby was from the Simon Crosby branch of the family. He went to Maine State College. He went with his mind made up to be an engineer. Oliver wrote poetry and music for students at Maine State. He also wrote articles for the local newspaper. They would send him to pick up the articles.

On graduating, Oliver worked on his family's farm, repairing fences and buildings along with building a few windmills. He also went to the Exposition in Philadelphia, which he could do because his folks paid him for his work. When Oliver got back home, he decided to go to St. Paul, Minnesota, where Simon Percy was living and working as an attorney. Oliver worked for a couple of years, and then founded the American Hoist and Derrick Company. Today, the company employs 700 people.

We were never a political family, despite several men

of prominence who held political office. For example, we had a William G. Crosby, a Whig, who was the twenty-third governor of Maine in 1853-55. We had Russel Wilder who was governor of Illinois. There were several constables who were Crosbys, and a couple of state representatives by the name of Crosby. Also, Ira Crosby, sheriff of Peoria County, Illinois, hired Abraham Lincoln to resolve a long-time problem for the family.

For Crosby history of a more recent and more personal nature, my basketball jersey was the first retired by Drury College in Springfield, Missouri. Here is what it says on the Drury website:

#44 Charlie Crosby (1952-1956)

A native of Branson, Missouri, Charlie was Drury's first 1,000 point scorer and its first basketball player to earn NAIA All-American honors. He was also a First Team All-MCAU selection and was nominated to join the USA Olympic All-Star team. He graduated from Drury in May of 1956 with 1,034 career points (now #33 on the Drury all-time scoring list) after scoring 498 points his senior season.

The retirement of a jersey is an honor reserved for people who perform beyond the call of duty, those who make unusual plays, or get unusual rebounds, or make unusual shots, or make unusually high percentages of shots. Don Fleshy announced in chapel that my jersey was being retired, but he didn't announce any of my other accomplishments. There was an All-American recognition, and a recognition of the most points in one game, 40, as a senior. There was a recognition of my invitation to play in the Petroleum Oil 66 Amateur League and an invitation to try out for the 1956 Olympic basketball team.

However, I didn't mind. I was injured and I was tired and I was just saying no to playing more basketball. I was receptive to other kinds of achievement, but would have to wait to see if others would be offered.

Hall of Fame usually goes with a little experience about ten years after graduation. Dr. Bruce Harger got after mine and moderated my entry into the Hall of Fame at Drury. I am eager to see the Shanahan brothers inducted into the Missouri Sports Hall of Fame for the three brothers, Dave, Phil, and Jim. It is now time for Branson to have their inclusion into the hall. I have guessed the criteria close enough.

I have spent several years growing up and living in the Ozarks as an athlete. I am in the sports hall of fame at Drury College. We do have the Missouri Sports Hall of Fame with the facility here in Springfield. While sports has been a big part of my life, I don't think we should put sports ahead of our good businessman here in the Ozarks. I think the best we can do is place them on equal footing here in the Ozarks, not limiting any hall of fame performers to sports. So far, as recognizing and remembering outstanding people we have in business as well as any other department, industry, or field that we can think of.

We can think of the different types of business as well as agriculture not to exclude architecture, engineering, medicine, or your professions. They should not be excluded from this selection. All business and professional men and women should be included in this hall of honoring.

In the business hall, we should consider businesses like the big beverages and food industries, including dairy products, frozen foods, meat, bread, pastries, potato chips, and deli. How about your over-the-counter fast foods and table services like McDonalds, Wendy's, Steak n' Shake, to mention just a few. Another type of fast food is the convenience stores where you can gas your car, such as Casey's, Robert's, Conoco, and others.

Let's not forget Pizza Hut and Pizzeria. This helps to encircle the food industry. Let's also not forget the Dairy Queens and the Braham's. We've got manufacturers, wholesalers, jobbers, and retailers who do such great work.

Isn't it great to have service clubs to take care of a vast number of business people. The Rotary, the Kiwanis, and the Metro, to mention a few.

We are thinking of a select few and should look to some of these clubs to make recommendations for the Business Hall of Fame.

The aforementioned probably does not name all deserving of an honoring in a hall of fame, but it serves as some example and ideas.

Other fields of business such as attractions for entertainment like theaters help millions of people every year enjoy themselves even if it is just for a few hours. The outdoor parks, like those in Branson and Eureka Springs, have been very beneficial in servicing the local populations as well as vacationers. There are several more indoor theaters. There was one that bordered on greatness and then Andy Williams passed on and made room for a few more. Bass Pro Shop jumped in to entertain a million or more people annually at their stores. Then add the World of Wonders museum which may handle another million guests. We still have the good, better, best park in Silver Dollar City, the fun park of the Ozarks, even though the big parks, Six Flags in St. Louis and Worlds of Fun in Kansas City, still give it a run.

I don't feel confident to discuss fishing even for the sake of the fishermen who come into this region for fishing. My three brothers go fishing on a regular basis and would be much more equipped to talk about fishing. There is also a man by the name of Charley Campbell who is an expert with the rod and reel and is also the best teacher at Bass Pro Shop. He ranks as one of the five top teachers in the Ozarks region. Anyone who wants a good day of learning, they should talk to Charley.

My next book will be a vacation guide by where all advertising is expected to be free for all businesses. That is all I am going to reveal at this time. I plan also to have another book similar to this one. I will reveal more information later on regarding my other book ideas. I expect to have a not-for-profit corporation to handle some business concerns in the future.

Books About Crosby History

Many books containing histories of various Crosby family members are available online. Some can be found at major online retailers such as Amazon and Barnes and Nobel. Others require more digging to find, but they are worth the effort. Most of these family histories were written more than 100 years ago and the manuscripts have fallen into the Public Domain. Several companies exist to maintain these records and make them available to modern-day readers, but most of the original manuscripts can be found for free, again, if the end justifies the means, meaning whether the reader is willing to dig.

One such manuscript is *Two Crosby Families*, written by Simon Percy Crosby and published in 1912 by The H. W. Kingston Company, St. Paul, Minnesota. It is but one example of the quality and character of the many Crosby families that have done so much to benefit their communities over the years.

Also recommended is *Simon Crosby, the Emigrant: His English Ancestry, and Some of His American Descendants,*

referred to so often here. *The Emigrant* was written by
Eleanor Davis Crosby and published by G. H. Ellis
Company, Boston, in 1914.

Another document of interest, although elusive, is the
history of Eliza Ann Miller and Cortes Fernando Crosby.
This manuscript contains 16 pages of local Crosby history
followed by a detailed 38-page listing of Crosby
genealogy, beginning with John Crosby in 1440 England
and ending with my generation in the late 1950s. Our
family is listed on page 38, when Floyd Peter Crosby
married Alvenia Bryant. This collection is more
meaningful to me because it touches only lightly on our
distant family from long ago and focuses on family that
settled in the Midwestern United States, especially around
Coy, Missouri. The approximate time period covered is
1850 to 1950. I have been unable to trace the origins of
this document, as the first four pages are missing. There
is a photo of Fernando Cortes Crosby and Eliza Ann
(Lide) Miller, with five other people, mostly Crosbys. The
final page includes a photo of Joshua H. Miller and his
wife, with what appears to be a name plate, A. Hinkel &
Son, Warrensburg, Mo. It is an interesting read, and I
continue to search for the source.

Yet a little while we linger,
Ere we reach our journey's end;
Yet a little while of labor,
Ere the evening shades descend;
Then we'll lay us down to slumber,
But the night will soon be o'er;
In the bright, the bright forever,
We shall wake, to weep no more.

Fanny Crosby
The Bright Forever

Made in the USA
San Bernardino, CA
29 November 2016